ENTER THE INFINITE

[THE PATH OF REALIZATION]

JAMES VAN GELDER

PUBLISHED BY JAMES VAN GELDER

Cover design by Tiberius Viris
http://www.Tiberius-Viris.com/

First Edition

All quotes by Tian De are included in the book with direct permission.

Enter the Infinite: The Path of Realization, is formally registered under the
United States Copyright Office.

ISBN 13: 978-0996192910
ISBN 10: 0996192913

The more expanded you are,

the less of a bind you are in.

-Tian De

AWAKENING
[the multi-dimensional being]

From a societal perspective, many are often expected to act both happy and content in order to fit in. However, as a result of this, many people in society are trying to emulate true happiness, even though happiness is not an action, but a natural reaction. The act of trying is a forced measure in order to replicate a natural phenomenon. Thus, a hollow and awkward state, one lacking feeling, is achieved. Some, however, effortlessly convey a state of excitement, embodying an authentic expression which can be felt by those around them. It is a pure wakefulness emerging from moment to moment; an expression of being truly alive.

In life, one is simply going from one situation to another and absorbing information and experiences along the way. Each new situation entered and experienced is like a slide being rotated on a projector screen, with every new slide bringing a new experience. However, during the presentation of one's life, it is possible that one may notice that the projector itself upgrades, similar to exchanging an old light bulb for a newer and more powerful one. Each upgrade bringing with it an increased level of brightness and quality to each new consecutive slide.

When considering the experience of life, many often approach the understanding of consciousness from a dualistic perspective. Individuals are often simply referred to as conscious or as unconscious. However, when considering the malleability of one's perception it becomes apparent that consciousness, an individual's state of being, has degrees of potential or intensities of wakefulness.

We don't see things as they are.

We see things as we are.

–Anaïs Nin

Shakyamuni, "Buddha," once explained to his disciple Ananda that beings exist on different levels, and although they may look at the same thing, they will actually see each thing according to their own perspective.[1] Similar to Einstein's *Theory of Relativity* where time is stretched and expanded relative to an object's density, an individual's experiential quality or perception also expands and shifts with relation to their choices and lifestyle. If happiness is ultimately a state of mind, the evolution perception is the focus of self-development. Because no matter where you place the dissatisfied, ghostly individual, their happiness is unlikely and, if anything, it is a fleeting joy.

When unaware of the malleability and development of one's perception it becomes habitual for one to take a stance towards life that is centered around food, shelter, and sexual intercourse: the characteristics of an animal. They are raised to believe that there is no greater achievement than survival. And that following the heart is unnecessary and illogical. For many, the guiding force in life is logic and rationality; a seemingly "safe" path based on human understanding and intellect. However, harboring such certainty may cause the awareness of the experience itself to become compromised along an apparently "rational" path.

"Logic, if you stick to logic you cannot go very far. What is logic other than the conventional way of thinking at a particular time and place? Our concern is with Logos, Reason, Truth which are beyond time and space."

–Daskalos[2]

It takes care to realize that one has the ability to evolve from a conscious perspective and expand the quality of one's life: a pursuit of greater understanding. A higher dimension to life exists beyond simply surviving, and the experience is the reward for being spiritual. Having no awareness of the possibility for greater depths of realization, fear-based obedience becomes habitual and day-to-day the spirit is not exercised. This is referred to as psychosis (soul sleep), because the aspect of one's self that is connected with self-refinement and growth is disregarded, and gradually one settles into a slower state requiring less concentration.

"Religion is a state of realization."

–Ziad

Truth seekers and yogis are the ones who are aware of the mutable aspect of their state of being and are taking a step in an effort to expand their experience as they progress through each new slide during life. These seekers notice the connection between the internal and the external and are making a conscious effort to upgrade the light bulb behind their perception by consciously choosing directions and situations in life that connect with their inner self.

"I'm not here to tell you the truth, I am here to help you find the truth. Because if I tell it to you, it is still just some words, you have

to find it yourself."

–Osho

It is ignorance that allows people to believe that true knowledge can be simply handed to them. Those that follow truth and self-refinement begin to 'see' the world differently. Instead of survival, life becomes about seeking truth. Along the way, these individuals will be experiencing shifts or upgrades in their present experience. The expansiveness of each present moment becoming continually intensified and clarified; more and more they bring an evolved state of being into each new situation in the future. Eventually, the overall experience of life in each new situation can be enhanced and brightened to such a degree that they escape suffering regardless of their external circumstances. These individuals serve as a powerful lighthouse guiding others towards the light, realizing that darkness is utilized as a function. They are known as buddhas. This level of awakening is known as buddhahood, arhat, completing the great work, theosis, gnosis, and enlightenment.

1 *Tibetan Wheel of Life* [11]

The Bhavacakra

The Tibetans teach that, ordinarily, man is in a constant state of suffering, stuck in what is known as samsara: a repeated cycle of life, death, and rebirth. Often credited with being created by the Buddha himself, the Bhavacakra, also known as the Tibetan Wheel of Life, illustration is a symbolic representation of samsara that was created in order to help people understand the Buddhist teachings.[1]

The Wheel of Life is spun by the Lord of Death, known as Yama. At the center of the wheel are the "Three Root Delusions" or the "Three Poisons," which represent the three faults that keep individuals spinning in the cycle of samsara. These are the three root illusions preventing individuals from self-realization. They represent greed, lust, and hatred and are depicted by a pig, rooster, and snake. The three poisons keep sentient beings from developing their spirit awareness in order to escape the constant spinning on the wheel of cyclic existence.

The Wheel of Life is split into six major sections, six realms of existence, each representing a certain type of suffering. On the upper half of the wheel are the demi-gods, gods, and humans. The gods and demi-gods have more than they need, and always get what they want, however, and because of this, they gain no determination or insight into existence and remain in a state of torpor. In addition, the demi-gods are always at war with the gods because of jealously. Occupying the lower half of the wheel, are the animals, hell-beings, and hungry ghosts. These beings are in a constant state of survival-based mentality, suffering, and fear (respectively), so great that they are prevented from gaining a deeper understanding of reality.

The human realm is not perfect and is characterized with some level of suffering such as aging, sickness, and death. However, because this realm is not completely filled with suffering or ease, a balance is formed and it is considered the most ideal place for following the dharma and gaining a deeper insight into reality. In this way, the Tibetans insist that there must be darkness in order for a person to find enlightenment. A sense of duality, like the lotus flower rising from muddy waters. It is because the human's reality is not perfect, but also not completely malevolent that they have the best opportunity to steadily rise towards enlightenment. Interestingly enough, because of the opportunity available in the human realm, if the Tibetan monks do not believe that they will achieve enlightenment in this lifetime they will actually pray to be reborn a human in the next life. It is for dharma that they have no desire to be reborn in the demi-god or god realms.

"The path to enlightenment seems dark."

–Lao Tzu

Outside of the wheel on the upper left is depicted a moon, or in this case a land of buddhas; this is a representation of liberation or enlightenment, the existential state breaking one free from cyclic existence. There is also Shakyamuni Buddha (upper right) who is pointing towards the moon/land of buddhas, signifying that everyone has the capability to reach enlightenment. The path leading to the moon is "The Way;" the path of self-refinement leading one towards a deeper experiential understanding of reality.

The Wheel of Life – A Psychological Perspective

While the six realms of sentient beings are seen as actual realms of existence by the Tibetans, the wheel can also be interpreted as a metaphor for the different levels of psychological states that an individual can experience during their human life. By falling prey to one or more of the three root delusions, the individual will be psychologically inhabiting one of the six realms of suffering, keeping them from consciously evolving.

"At this moment, if we are mindful of Bodhisattvas and of cultivating the Six Paramitas, we are in the Bodhisattva realm. Similarly, if we are mindful of virtue, morality, and humanity, we are in the human realm. But, if we are greedy, constantly scheming to make money and to possess materialistic enjoyments, we are in the hungry ghost realm. If our thinking is confused and deluded, and we are drifting along through life, we are in the animal realm. And if we are displeased and angry with everyone and everything, we are in the hell realm."

–Chin Kung[2]

Six Paramitas: Generosity, Wisdom that discriminates, Meditative concentration, Joyful Endeavour, Patience, Discipline, Generosity.[3]

The upper three sufferings of the human, god, and demi-god realms are commonly associated with impermanence, pride, and jealousy, while the lower three sufferings are fear, pain, and deprivation.

The hungry ghost realm is inhabited by round beings that have tight narrow necks that only allow a small amount of sustenance to enter, preventing them from ever being able to get their fill. While the hungry ghosts are perpetually hungry, their bodies are very round and obese, implying that a lack of food is not the source of their hunger. Metaphorically, this is a representation of a person that has lost contact with his or her true self, the bringer of life, causing them to feel perpetually empty on the inside. As they are always feeling empty on the inside, no amount of external sustenance can satisfy them. They are round because no matter how much they eat; they always feel hungry for more. On a side note, it is somewhat interesting, as far as my understanding, that one of the most scientific correlations regarding long life is the habit of eating less. However, those that are full on life will do this naturally.

> "Eat to live, don't live to eat."
> -Tian De

No place on the wheel is the true goal, and every place on the wheel has the propensity for reaching the true goal; the capability to escape samsara and reach enlightenment in each realm is illustrated by the Buddha with a halo that can be seen in each realm. No matter if one is rich or poor, a god or suffering in hell, their quality and potential towards true happiness, a state of divinity, is the same distance.

Two monks observe a flag swaying in the wind.

The first monk asks the other monk,

"What is moving?

Is it the flag, or the wind?"

The second monk says,

"Neither,

it is your mind that is moving."

Intelligence & Intellect

In society today, many consider intelligence and intellect to be synonymous, simply defining both words as meaning smart. While both are necessary, there exists a fundamental difference between the two.

Intellect

Intellect shapes the content of what one thinks; it is the information one obtains. When looking at a computer, intellect can relate to the software or the programs that are installed. These programs that have been downloaded are not perfect and eventually become outdated requiring the need for them to be upgraded regularly.

Intellect is often gained through reading books or studying in school. When the common education system approaches the process of learning, they are addressing the intellectual side: a dissemination of information and ideas, collected and organized for the focus of a particular discipline. The series of ideas that are presented are accepted by the community and are seen as important for each student's understanding.

The problem with intellect is that it is bound to the relative and at a degree of separation with reality. One's current level of comprehension is the foundation for the formulation of intellect. For example, if one considers a dog's understanding relative to a human's, primary thoughts such as food and water that a dog contemplates will seem rudimentary to the average human. On the other hand, a human concept such as multiplication would seem to be on an entirely different dimension of understanding for a dog. This large gap of feasible conceptualization between the dog and the human illustrates how the depth of intellect is bound by the bearer's capacity. When compared with a theoretical higher intelligence, one beyond that of a human, the limited nature of a human's intellect would also become equally apparent.

"Relative and absolute, these the two truths are declared to be. The absolute is not within the reach of the intellect, for the intellect is grounded in the relative."

–Shantideva 9.2

Taking into account the limited, circumstantial, and non-encompassing nature of intellect, how should one go about authentically reaching true understanding? How does one reach the absolute? For this, one must go beyond the intellect and into the realm of the experience itself.

Intelligence

The two words intellect and intelligence would be synonymous if there was not a deeper component of oneself beyond the human body with the potential for development. Where intellect relies on human reasoning, the source of intelligence is found in experiential quality. The difference between intelligence and intellect is what separates great individuals from the average.

Intelligence is intensity; simply put, it is the level of one's concentration. True knowledge and understanding of the world comes from the depth of the experience. One does not need books or study to increase intelligence. One cannot be given a "bright mind," because it is an existential aspect, related to intensity, which must be earned and developed.

"Study," he said, "is of no use in gaining true knowledge, it is rather an obstacle. All that we learn in that way is in vain. In fact, one only knows one's own ideas and one's own visions. As for the real causes that have generated these ideas they remain inaccessible to us. When we try to grasp them we only seize the ideas that we, ourselves, have elaborated about these causes."

–Sakyong Gomchen[1]

Considering the depth of one's realization is the highest form of truth, those who are aware of this aspect, and are working to expand it, are increasing intelligence.

When considering the electronics metaphor, intelligence can be seen as the actual computer itself. Increasing intelligence is increasing every functional component of the computer, a comprehensive upgrade.

Some may occasionally cross paths with individuals who appear seemingly perfect in all aspects. However, it is not a coincidence that every aspect of these individuals is operating in complete harmony. There is a source behind this harmony that guides and organizes the totality of one's being. This organizing force is sometimes referred to as the spirit-soul, a quality pervading every operation and function of one's being, reaching far beyond the cellular level. This unobstructed guidance organizes higher efficiency in one's being, creating an abundance of health, beauty, and wakefulness. While these individuals are somewhat rare, they are a product of natural evolution. The development of this "inner" aspect is intelligence. These individuals are closer to reality and in a deeper communion with existence than average people, moving every aspect of their being towards perfection: memory, health, happiness, appearance.

Where intellect is prized in the west, intelligence is worshipped in the east. From a normal perspective, unaware of intelligence, the practice of meditation, usually seen as a type of religious devotion, appears seemingly irrational and faith based. However, meditation is going beyond one's relative intellect in order to develop a source of life connected with experiential clarity. In Indian philosophy, experiential wisdom is known as jnana: a cognitive event which is recognized when experienced. It is knowledge inseparable from the total experience of reality, especially a total or divine reality.[2] The yogis and alchemists are not studying existence with external microscopes or laboratories, but instead are working to heighten and expand the awareness which is perceiving the reality before them in order to gain a deeper understanding of existence. When understanding this pursuit, the reverence that many Asian cultures place on their enlightened masters becomes comprehensible. Who can know more about existence than one whose perception is so deeply purified? Their experience is incomprehensible and cannot be explained with words. Self-refinement towards divinity cannot be given by another, as highlighted by the Tibetan Bhavacakra, not even the wealthy can achieve it without effort.

"Again I tell you, it is easier for a camel to go through the eye of a needle than for someone who is rich to enter the kingdom of God."

–Matthew 19:24

Increasing intellect will only get one so far because one's understanding is limited by the receiver's current level of intelligence (the computer itself). True intelligence is an aspect of development that the majority of schools and organizations are not yet aware of. In a way it is heaven's secret.

What is the consequence of institutions not being aware of intelligence? The problem is not as much that the influx of information will eventually become outdated, but that it can actually begin to overload the system itself. If there are too many programs running at the same time on a particular computer, the computer itself will begin to slow down. Similarly, an individual can begin to slow down in reality when there is too much on their mind.

"As I get older, I begin more and more to feel that being brought up and "educated" is a form of hypnosis, brainwashing, and indoctrination that is extremely difficult to survive with one's senses intact."

–Alan Watts

It is important to note that Alan Watts was very well acquainted with the academic world. He was a graduate-school dean, a professor, and a Harvard University research fellow.[3] With no desire to exercise intelligence, multifaceted cramming can cause an individual to lose touch with the malleability of the conscious experience: the source of life.

"Protect your mind."

–Tian De

When the awareness is clouded, life can be like walking in darkness, the individual may have a high degree of intellect, but they have no situational awareness. It is common to become argumentative and easily agitated: the ego overcoming the presence.

The answer is to increase intelligence. When the computer has too much software and is slowing down and freezing, it is time to purchase a more powerful one. By increasing intelligence one is gaining clarity and embodying a state of ease; it is working with the source of life within, a nourishment that cannot come from food or sleep.

"If a man neglects education, he walks lame to the end of his life."
–Plato

Intellect and intelligence can work in harmony, if one is learning what they have an interest in. A synergy is created between the two, as the subject material brings the individual closer to the present moment.

[Psychedelics]

Lucid dreaming, is the phenomenon of becoming self-aware during the course of one's dream. The individual may be going through a variety of abstract events, but then suddenly they gain a flash of insight that causes them to realize that they are in fact dreaming from a mind-state that is beyond the experiences around them: a realization of a deeper truth that penetrates the very fabric of their circumstantial reality.

However, what is more important than becoming self-aware during a dream, is becoming experientially lucid during the course of one's life.

Many traditions around the world have incorporated psychedelics in "awakening ceremonies" for this very reason: to reveal the path of yoga.[4] By artificially stimulating the brain, psychedelics have the ability to peel back the layers of perception and push an individual into a more awakened state conscious awareness, thus allowing them to gain a deeper understanding of reality.[5] Because the path of yoga naturally increases the intensity of life, altered states induced by substances are intimately connected with spiritual research.

Lineages that utilize psychedelics do not view them as simply "bad" but, instead like a powerful sword that is only to be wielded carefully and with purpose. When taken at the appropriate dosage, the mind-altering substances are utilized as a tool for initiation in order to open "doors" of perception previously inaccessible to the student; thereby allowing the student to gain an understanding on an experiential level of the importance of the path of inner truth that would ordinarily not be comprehensible.

"The Psychedelic experience is only a glimpse of genuine mystical insight, but a glimpse which can be matured and deepened by the various ways of meditation in which drugs are no longer necessary or useful. If you get the message, hang up the phone. For psychedelic drugs are simply instruments, like microscopes, telescopes, and telephones. The biologist does not sit with eye permanently glued to the microscope, he goes away and works on what he has seen."

–Alan Watts

One does not need substances to get high on life, but the substances can show a person what it means to be high on life.

If the brain is sufficiently stimulated naturally, mind-altering substances will have no effect. There is story where Ram Dass, an American spiritual teacher, brings LSD with him on his trip to India. During his trip he meets with Guru Maharajji. Maharajji asks Ram Dass if he can see the "medicine" that he brought with him. Ram Dass empties the LSD, which are in pill form, on his hand and then much to his surprise, Maharajji quickly grabs and eats them. He eats a total of twelve hundred micrograms of LSD, which is four times the normal dosage for an average person. However, an hour passes by and much to Ram Dass's amazement Maharajji is no different and is still the same. Maharajji then explains how this type of medicine will have no effect on those who have their mind fixed towards God.[6] Through self-refinement, Maharajji had already awaked the areas of the brain that LSD stimulates; he was already lucid.

"Wanting to take a shortcut to a relationship with God, I think that is where the name getting high comes from."

–Anthony Kiedis[7]

Because the effects are not lasting, and that continual use of these substances can result in structural damage, they cannot be considered a genuine path. From what I have noticed, those who use substances regularly actually begin to lose touch with reality. They lose their discipline and edge in life, and actually begin to fall asleep in a way.

It is unfortunate when people chase a higher experiential quality, a state of divinity, through psychedelics because they are unaware that a true path exists. Those addicted to realization, like the yogis, understand the hidden aspects of life that many people may never comprehend. One normal lifetime of experiences expanded into a hundred lifetimes of experiences: the result of wakefulness.

WORK

Through the expression of work, we earn our rewards.

Work is a primary method of self-expression in fulfilling all obligation to support ourselves.

Through work, we can contribute to the collective good of society & the evolution of man.

Work is an essential part of self-expression and self-preservation.

Work will increase our value to others.

WORK & SUCCESS

As a young man passed through a street, he saw a rich man giving alms to a beggar. The young man thought to himself, "God is great. He provides to all and takes care of all. As I'm made in His image, a child of God, then for certain, God will take care and provide for me."

He went home, sat and did nothing, waiting for God to provide. A week passed and nothing happened. Two weeks, then three, and still nothing happened. Soon, he was dying of starvation. A holy man passed by and asked him what had happened. With the little strength left in his body, he told his story.

The holy man said, "When you saw the two men, you should have learnt from the rich and not from the beggar.

The rich man provides for himself and also provides for others. Your success can help others, but your failures cannot. God helps those who help themselves.

WORK & LESSONS

There is no division between your daily work and your spiritual development.

Every situation will accelerate your spiritual evolution.

Through work, you will encounter beings and events that mirror your spiritual states and needs.

Through work, you will meet and encounter people and events that either irritates or uplift you.

The cosmic and universal intention utilizes these particular situations or challenges to teach us beneficial lessons for our highest good concerned.

The purpose of labor is to learn and earn. To learn how to live. And earn a living.

When you know it, the labor is over.

A flower blossoms to create fruit.

When that comes, the petal falls.

Work is our greatest Teacher

DO YOUR WORK

Work does not need you. You need work.

He who performed his prescribe duty however difficult it may seem, frees himself from the bondage of life.

Cosmic intelligence created this universe for us.

The universe does not need us. But we need the universe.

If anyone of us disappears from this planet, the planet will continue to exist.

If one planet disappears from this galaxy, the galaxy will continue to exist.

If our galaxy disappears from the universe, the universe will continue to exist.

Similarly, the work we do does not need us, but we need the work.

It really put our self-importance into a proper perspective.

The world does not need anything.
Everything is already there.

All necessities are already created in such great force that overcomes all human reasons.

There's nothing to create. Everything is already created for us. We just need to be creative with the created.

Our work is to discover our work.

And when you are true to your assigned work, your work is done.

WORK-NO ESCAPE

If you have great knowledge but you do nothing, your knowledge will do nothing to you.

This knowledge will be worthless and no meaning to you nor others.

Even a spiritualist or philosopher or even a scientist needs to do something about his skills or knowledge so that he himself and others can benefit from the profound discoveries, wisdom and realization.

The universe is ever-changing and acts unceasingly accordingly to the time, place, and circumstance.

An individual is ever active whether asleep, eating, or idle.

Even in the motionless deep sleep state, his internal bodies and systems are ever active... supporting his life, feeling, thoughts, and gestures etc.

An infant works unceasingly to learn the wonders of his new world.

A student works to acquire basic knowledge and skills of life.

An adult works to support a livelihood in himself and others.

An elder works to maintain the well-being of his body, contributing his experiences and knowledge to those who need guidance.

21

An old aged man works to contemplate the life behind him and the path before him.

The bottom line is… As long as you possess a body, you cannot escape work.

WORK WITH NATURE

The objectives of our work is to move more people from non-action into action and eventually from action to effective and constructive results.

Many people read all kinds of motivational books to overcome inertia. Yet, there are also a lot of people who simply grab hold of any books in the marketplace in the hope of improving their spiritual endeavors.

Cosmic intelligence has planned for every one of us. They planned and organized nature with prescribed timing accordingly to their natural habitat.

There's a time to plant. A time to harvest. A time for action. A time to wait.

If you do not understand these fundamental truth, and missed the planting season, you will have no crops for the whole year.

If you missed the harvesting season, you will have crops rotting in the field.

If you missed the time for fertilizing the crops, you will have a poor harvest for the year.

A rich harvest is dependent on the farmer's timely dedication to his work.

He does not need motivational books.

He lived with nature's abundance and timing.

WORK WITH INTUITION & GRACE

When we perform our work, we have to be silently in tune with our inner self for guidance.

Each one of us hears their inner silent voice differently.

To some, it comes naturally. Others must cultivate that intuition through various inner work & spiritual practices.

The definition of intuition according to the dictionary is as follows:

Direct perception of Truth, facts. Independent of any reasoning process. Pure, untaught, non-inferential knowledge, etc.

Intuition is extremely undervalued by many, yet, everyone who has ever succeeded in any extraordinary task has always drawn upon its power.

Many revolutionary scientific breakthroughs often begin with an intuitive perception of unknown potential.

A well-developed intuition is an invaluable tool.

The source of intuition is the same which provides inspiration to all great Masters.

However, we must know that the sixth sense (thought) is not intuition.

The six senses are evolved in the following sequence, feeling, odor, taste, sound, sight, and finally thought forms.

Intuition is the
In- or inner-tuition.

In other words, the inner introspection.

The esoteric work within.

The living divine self: teaching or giving us tuition inside.

This is our Maker's Grace, His favors, and His light to all of us.

Through his Grace, the Universe came into existence.

Through His Grace, beings are able to be inspired to perform their duties and maintain their functions.

This is our Gift, a Divine Grace.

Each one of us possesses that Grace within.

Some of us are in touch with it, while others are not.

Those who are irresponsible of their duty, and who hide away, will deprive themselves the Grace of the Divine Light.

Those responsible, sincere, Souls who immerse themselves in the warmth of The Divine Light, will receive full benefit from it.

WORK WITH DETACHMENT, SACRIFICE, WORSHIP & PERFECTION

Each one of us is unique.

What works for one does not necessarily work for others.

Try to find and discover your natural rhythm that works for you.

When your duty is performed with a sense of detachment, the very work performed becomes a sacrifice and a worship to our Maker.

Bring overly concerned with the rewards will never enhance the outcome of our work. Instead, it will interfere with our performance.

In other words, the success of winning is not about focusing on the winning but what you must do in order to win.
That's what it means to be detached.

Sacrifice is an act of offering.

An offering of our labor to the One who grants us the ability to act.

It is work without an attachment to self or sense gratifications.

Just by adopting this attitude, our efforts become a sacrifice to our creator.

Thus, the sacrifice serves as a worship.

Treating your work as a sacrifice and worship will not lessen your compensation.

Whatever rewards we deserve will be due to us.

This attitude will transform the ordinary task to something sacred.

It will change and enhance our performance into greater results: Into Perfection.

-Tian De

Note: Tian De's incorrect use of capitalization is an emphasis of the divine. He will often capitalize the word "Soul," and by doing so he is making the connection between one's soul and God.

"Concentration and meditation will not give power so long as ignorance remains. Desire and misery will recur until one masters the nature of things."

–Helen Rhodes[1]

One's choices and approach towards life is the determining factor for the continuance of spiritual growth. One's actions in life, dependent on order of precedence, will affect one's awakening.

"There are many paths toward our ascent to God. It is not only those who have been initiated into the mysteries who are searching. I am telling you that there are persons who have never heard of the phrase Research for Truth (Path for Enlightenment) and who may even be atheistic and yet at a higher step on the spiritual path than many of us. We should judge people not on the basis of their beliefs but on the basis of their actions. I am not aware of anyone who sincerely struggles toward the Truth who has not eventually been enlightened."

–Daskalos[2]

When viewing life challenges as being relevant to spiritual growth, the perpetuation of conscious realization, many traditions look towards detachment, or "ego-death," as necessary for an individual to be able to continually evolve. The ability to bend instead of break, and flow instead of crash. The ego death is a way to remove hindrance from responding to life's problem and allow the individual to continuously adapt and evolve. When going beyond the intellect and into the experience itself, fear is an obstacle.

"I must not fear. Fear is the mind-killer. Fear is the little-death that brings total obliteration. I will face my fear. I will permit it to pass over me and through me. And when it has gone past I will turn the inner eye to see its path. Where the fear has gone there will be nothing. Only I will remain."

-Frank Herbert[3]

In Buddhism, "Arhat" is the name often given to an individual that has entered Buddhahood, or liberation, while alive on earth; he or she is considered to be a self-realized and self-mastered being. However, when directly defined, the term Arhat means, "one who destroys the foes of affliction." It is one who is able to walk fearlessly into the obstacles that confront them, continually preserving spiritual awareness in the present moment. Instead of having a war occurring on the inside, he or she is confronting the external world in order to preserve internal clarity. In this regard, fear is often seen as an obstruction to self-mastery, an obstacle towards those that wish to retain control of the mind. The lust of self becomes the loss of self, hindering personal growth.

In the Warner Brothers film *The Matrix*, the main character, Neo, begins waking up to a deeper side of reality. His mentor, Morpheus, helps to show him the true nature of reality and guides him along his path towards realizing his potential as "the one." Morpheus explains to Neo that he was born into a prison that cannot be smelled or touched, a prison of the mind. Morpheus also explains to Neo that no one can be told what the matrix is and that he would have to see it for himself.[4]

Similar to the matrix, experiencing self-realization cannot be conceptualized and must be experienced. In reality, the prison that one cannot smell, or taste, or touch, is of the mind and is a direct result of a lack of self-mastery. When an individual does not have self-mastery, then they are unconsciously moving from thought to thought, experiencing a fogged perception. Every aspect of the experience is tarnished; it is a prison that one takes with them everywhere, remaining like an imperceptible splinter.

"The reason why mundane people are unable to attain sagehood is because they have too many wandering and false thoughts running through their minds."

–Yun Gu[5]

The "true mind," or the conscious awareness, is clouded behind the "deluded mind," commonly represented by wants, needs, and desires, hindering perception. The more expanded the awareness, or true mind, becomes with relation to the uncontrollable thoughts, or deluded mind, the more the conscious experience expands.[6]

HUMAN BEING

The way towards Self-Realization and Enlightenment is the process of becoming more and more human in one's perfect feelings, thoughts, and deeds.

To be more human is to be very humane.

A living being filled with the embodiment of compassion, a heart of love, and a mind of wisdom.

These are the leading steps towards our True Being.

And it should be every human being's aspiration.

A Buddha, a self-realized soul, an enlightened spirit being, an avatar, a master of truth, a transcendental being.

Totally different from the so-called normal human whose lives are spent no differently than an animal: eating, sleeping, mating, and defending.

All great souls were once upon a time human.

The Great One who encompasses great compassion, love, and wisdom for both living and non-living becomes The Most Extraordinary Being.

They have evolved to their True Being, a "perfect human being," and transcend ordinary humanity. They are known and referred to as, The Awakened One, Enlightened, Messiah, Master, etc.

It is from this human realm that we can steadily transform and transcend to be our "Truth" Being.

-Tian De

Religion

When looking at the origin of the word religion, the first part, Re, is a prefix which means to "return" and the second part, Ligion, comes from the Latin word, "ligare," which means "to bind." When put together, the two parts form the word religion. Religion is then more correctly translated as a "return to bondage." However, this form of bondage, is not necessarily meant to represent a negative situation. Instead, similar to a brace or a cast, religion can be looked at as a support for assisting a person back to clarity.

"Religion is like a walking stick. When you are young you need help from your parents to walk. When you are old you need a cane. When you are a healthy adult, you have no need for a cane; if you try to run, it will only hinder you. All religions are like that; touch God directly, and you will have no need of them."

–Teaching for John Chang[1]

Avoiding wrongdoing functions as a walking stick to experiential truth because with each step, one is reducing his or her entanglements and moving towards God: a more profound and deeper realization of reality. For many people in the West, reaching heaven is thought to be an actual location that one goes to in the afterlife; a perfect circumstance rewarded for living a moral life. In the East, reaching heaven is instead a quality that is realized while alive on Earth: a conscious state that permeates through external sufferings.

"Right now, as you are, you would be unhappy anywhere even in heaven. You will find ways and means of being unhappy there too, because you will carry all your jealousies, all your anger, all your greed, all your possessiveness. You will carry all your rage, all your sexuality, all your repressions; you will carry this whole luggage. The moment you reach heaven, you will create hell around yourself there too, because you will be carrying the seeds of hell.

It is said that if you are pure, if you are silent, you reach heaven. The truth is just the opposite: if you are pure, if you are silent, heaven reaches you. One never goes anywhere, one is always here, but once the inside becomes full of light the whole world outside is transformed."

—Osho[2]

Dissolving Destiny

In the West, the idea of destiny often represents an ideal situation, a path that is illuminated by a higher power. Individuals are destined by a higher power to become great. However, when looking at the idea of destiny in the East, specifically Chinese Buddhism, every individual has the capacity to become truly extraordinary. Destiny is instead the framework that encapsulates the individual; a circumstance that a person must overcome through appropriate action in order to expand their true potential, eventually becoming truly free: a liberation beyond destiny's wretch. For this reason, in Buddhism, it is said that whatever is properly sought can be attained.

"To the mind that is still, the whole universe surrenders."

–Lao Tzu

Every recurring idea or unaddressed aspect of a person's circumstance is seen as a mechanism that perpetually clouds the individual. A mechanism that must be addressed in order to reach a more profound state of silence-clarity.

Responsibility = Response Ability

When the Buddhists teach one to "abandon worldly desires," it does not mean to run away into the jungle, join an ashram, and lose all connection with society. To abandon worldly desires means to let go of one's attachment with the world in order to do what is necessary and maintain control of the senses. (citation, maybe?) It is a clinging to the world that is preventing the individual from destroying the foes of affliction. The world is seen as an illusion, because if one runs or hides, one carries hell within themselves. Abandoning worldly desires is to take hold of one's destiny and cultivate inner peace rather than waging a war within oneself.

"Those who hide away are denied the divine light."
–Tian De

Addressing the mechanisms is most commonly referred to as "correcting one's faults." Faults are determined by self-introspection, feeling, and observation. Finding one's faults requires observation of oneself in order to determine the stimulus that is clouding one's mental state.

"When cultivating the self, one should be aware of one's faults, and resolve
to correct them just as in curing a sickness. Perseverance is required, and
attainment comes when one's practice matures and ripens."
–Master Yun Gu[3]

True Buddhists are not primarily doing good deeds and correcting their faults in order to help others, but instead they are working to cultivate more profound states of realization. The path of destiny is a path of action that a person adheres to in order to return the mind to its natural state of purity. The habitual framework that defines the person is their destiny, a fixed mindset that one ordinarily does not escape.

"The body is the temple of God; the soul is God himself. If you pollute your own body and it deteriorates, and your brain disintegrates, God will naturally leave your body. But if you know enough to sacrifice, you will reach a certain rewarding stage. Then you'll give up all that is 'nice,' easy to get, and 'fun,' and you'll eventually purify your body. That is like cleaning and repainting a temple to await God's entrance."

-Kwan Saihung[4]

The framework of a person's destiny is believed to be connected with an individual's karma. Therefore, whatever actions that lead the individual to a deeper state of silence is viewed as the will of heaven.[5] By taking care of one's responsibilities, the person is creating an alchemical balance with nature, dissolving both mental and physical entanglements. Eventually, when the "no-mind" state of self-mastery is finally attained, it is then that an individual is beyond the sage's prediction and has transcended their destiny: they are truly free.

While many might view Buddhism as a religion of faith, Buddhism approaches an individual's destiny almost like a video game, with an intensely mathematical rationale behind it. Buddhism and Taoism are speaking of action. They are not relying on blessings, but are *creating* blessings. It is not belief in faith, but rather belief in scientific principles of reality that guide existence. It is said that a great sage is able to predict a person's future just by observing them for a short period of time. The sage observes every aspect of the individual: every small gesture, and every movement.[6]

SILENCE

Silence enfolds the nature of the cosmic universe.

To the sages and initiates, to every sensible human being, silence is a sign of perfection.

Silence is a sign that everything is functioning smoothly in an organism.

The organs of a healthy body are silent.

Silence is a language of perfection.

Whereas noise is the expression of a defect or anomaly or a life which is still unorganized and anarchical and still needs to be tamed and elaborated.

The quest for silence is an inner process which leads human beings to the light and to a true understanding of things within and without.

Realizing this, one can then seek silence in order to give his/her heart, soul, and spirit the opportunity to manifest themselves through meditations, prayers, and philosophical or artistic creation.

Without silence, all meditations, prayers, etcetera... will have no effects.

Silence is the expression of peace, calm, harmony, and perfection.
To live an active luminous life of peace, harmony, calm, and perfection, one must learn to love silence.

And one must also learn to pursue silence, to attain silence, to achieve silence.

It is possible to be silence.[1]

The noisy person whose life is filled with guilts, egos, mistrust, suspicion, and pride will have a hard time being silent. They are constantly in the infernal noises of hankering and lamentation.

It is possible to achieve an inner state of silence.

For silence is a quality of the inner life.

Silence is not an emptiness.

To be silent does not mean to sit in a quiet room and isolate yourself from the world.

You must perform your duties with peace harmony and perfection.

Whether you're a housewife, a worker, a disciple, initiate, spiritual worker, charity volunteer, preacher, laborer, boyfriend, girlfriend, brother or sister, etc...

If you can perform your work peacefully without attachment and conditioning, and if you do it with love and peace, not bothered by the money and pride, suspicion and mistrust.

SILENCE can delay but cannot deny you.

And if you're not affected by unfair criticism, cheating, lies, gossips and rumors, you can attain silence easily.

Silence is not an emptiness.
It's not an inertia, nothingness, void, or the absence of all activities.

No one can be empty.

Many religious faiths preach emptiness, voidness, or nothingness, etc.

They're impractical and absurd.

The silence of a higher degree of life is the Stillness that surrounds the great intensity of perfect harmony, a fullness within the body Spirit Soul amongst the ever turbulent society.

We do not have to hide in the jungle mountain caves and away from society.

Whether you're living alone or in a family or in an ashram, you can achieve silence if you can take charge of your emotions and responsibility.

This means that in order to be inwardly silent, you must create harmony in your physical body, thoughts, feelings, and gestures.

-Tian De

NATURAL PROGRESSION
[Self-Refinement through Concentration]

Cultivating silence through introspection, handling the mundane, and refraining from evil ideally creates the environment necessary to become in touch with the inner spirit-soul. Becoming aware of conscious evolution occurring within oneself, the next step is to continually make an effort to facilitate the process of expansion through self-refinement/concentration. Some refer to this as "following the heart," or simply being in touch with the true self.

The hidden truth behind following the heart is that it creates silence, a state of peace, allowing the awareness to expand to new dimensions. This is also known by some as entering "heart space." From this perspective, one continues to grow and expand from the heart. Not coincidentally, in the embryo, the heart plays a central role in the development of the physical body. While the body is forming, it actually begins as a heart and then grows outwardly from there.

'The ultimate goal is to realize who you are, to become one with God, to become a god. This is what we call Theosis. We are gods, but we are not aware of it. We suffer from a self-inflicted amnesia. The aim is to reawaken that which we have always been and we shall always be."

–Daskalos[1]

It is a process of re-awakening our immortal nature, and experiencing the infinite. Conscious shifting experiences, while similar to the effect of certain drugs, are a natural result of one's experiential expansion, a stimulation of the nervous system. The "true mind" penetrating the "deluded mind."

SELF-REALIZATION

"Self-realization is knowing who you are.

Your true self is your real self, the realized self.

The sole purpose of life comes from our soul.

Therefore, our sole purpose in life is to know that giver of life.

That giver of life is none other than our Soul.

She is very intimate to our True Self.

And she's the Soul mate of the True Self.

The soul mate helped me realize my true self of Who I am.

She has an intimate relationship with my true Self.

And knowing the Soul, you will get to know the True self.

In other words, you will only be Realizing your true self when you are connected to your Soul.

That's who I am.
"I am that I am."

That's who you are.
And you are always you.

Without the Soul mate, there's no chance for self-realization. And without self-realization, nothing is possible.

When you discover your Soul mate, she will introduce you to her ultimate boyfriend within.

That Ultimate boyfriend is our Spirit.

And he will welcome you warmly and light up your life's path.

The Fire of the soul and the light of the spirit burns so brightly together, merging as a luminous Twin Flame.

This Twin Flames lights up the True Self with such luminosity and purity, transforming you into an Enlightenment being.

The fiery lights of the enlightened being continue to burn intensely within with such intensity and force that it annihilates and frees us from all the emotional, causal, astral, egotistical, and karmic imprints and debris since time immemorial. "

-Tian De

     The way that one knows they are connecting with their true self and making evolutionary progress, is that they begin to experience themselves in new dimensions of awareness. The lens through which reality is experienced shifts, and with this shift brings a higher perception and understanding of existence. Connection directly with the soul. Instead of creating silence by handling responsibility and refraining from evil, soul-purpose directly creates silence and perpetuates a state of self-realization. This is following the light, and ultimately, light is the ability to see.

"To seek mind with the discriminating mind is the greatest of all mistakes."

–Seng–Ts'an

     This is similar to the Zen Buddhist's real-mind/stained-mind. Those that experience expansion, self-realization, and self-remembering are operating from the real mind or the "mind" as referenced to in the quote above. Those creating restriction to their awareness are operating in the discriminating mind. (The idea behind Buddhist Destiny is to minimize the activity of the discriminating mind.)

"What is important is that in each moment I am focused on that technique, I lose myself in it and enter into a state of mushin [literally "no mind"]. This type of training is a form of Zen training, more specifically the Soto Zen [the school of Zen Buddhism founded by Dogen Zenji]. Zen Buddhism teaches that the truth [of your existence] can only come from yourself. And can only be achieved through forgetting your own self [ego]. In order to forget your own self, you must have a singular concentration on the moment which requires you to remove all other distractions or obstacles. When you can achieve mushin you have removed all distractions and have perfect concentration and are able to see the truth for what it is."

–Murakami Katsumi

It is both silence and concentration that a space is created, a freedom where all the minds chatter begins to slow down and experientially bring a person into the present moment. "Mushin" is the awakening experience—that which brings inter-dimensional insight.

"If your right eye causes you to sin, take it out and throw it away. It is much better for you to lose a part of your body than to have your whole body thrown into hell."

[Mathew 5:29]

The word "sin" has been wrongly understood by many. From the original Hebrew, to sin actually means, "to miss the mark." It does not mean to do something bad, but instead means to miss one's true potential. Sinning is a lack of self-discovery. Jesus was not violent, instead he was trying to illustrate the importance of being in a state of self-realization. Hell in this quote, is a state without a connection to the spirit. By missing one's mark, one throws their whole body into hell.

"It is not a question of discovering the "I" but of expressing it. This is the purpose of the Research for Truth, to find out who you are and to express yourself as you ought to."

–Daskalos[2]

Knowing one's true self is only the beginning. In order to evolve, one needs to continually express oneself, the path of refinement. It is through the expression, or the doing, that a person clarifies and raises their conscious experience. Therefore, it takes commitment and persistence to evolve and pull the heavenly experience down to earth.

Soul-Survival

In life there is no escaping work, everyone has to work, and one cannot go without work for very long. Without work, beyond the diminishing of one's money, an individual's health and mental well-being will also begin to fade away: gravity brings destruction. Because there is no escape, it almost makes sense that Buddhists insist humans are actually of a low rank when compared with the larger spectrum of sentient beings.[3]

"Never have too little or too much."

–Lao Tzu.

From the standpoint that one always has to be of service, an important aspect of life can be finding a duty that enriches the spirit-soul. In this way, one's spiritual practice is connected with their regular duty, making for a powerful combination: the idea of success shines in a new light. That of being self-sufficient through a method of self-refinement can be considered a higher form of success. Work becomes a purpose that extends beyond one's survival, and connects with one on an existential level. Focusing on survival, many jobs today are judged by their paycheck, instead of the actual doing. However, instead of looking towards saving up for the future, sometimes an effort to try and escape work, the alchemist transforms their method of service into a tool for refining their concentration: soul-purpose. In this way, the alchemist harnesses the darkness in order to create light, a path of using one's perceived enemy in order to defeat their true enemy.

Traditionally the path towards discovering a work that connects with the inner spirit-soul (soul-purpose) is a natural one.

The Grandmaster said,

"The first requirement for learning the Way is hard work; then you need to learn to be a member of society, which means doing good and refraining from evil, building up character. When you have developed virtue and built up character, eventually you enter naturally into the Way."[4]

Finding a form of "soul purpose" is as simple as working. A common expression is, "work to find your work." Whether someone has discovered a form of "soul purpose" in life or not, if they work and refrain from evil, tradition teaches that they will be moving towards discovering, from the soul, a purpose. One may notice that people often change their career paths after they have started working because they are evolving and moving towards a greater purpose.

A person knows when they have found a work that connects with their spirit-soul because it creates stillness in the midst of life's chaos, a palpable step towards the infinite experience.

"Those who work hard live long,

Those who follow Dao live forever."

–Lao Tzu

"The Way," a term coined by the ancient Daoists, involves a path of evolving perception leading one towards conscious immortality and nirvana. Dao is the endless journey inward, it is the path of being connected with one's soul, the giver of life. The soul is The Way, and the path is illuminated by the expanding experience. Everyone has direct access to the giver of life inside of them, and as such, there are no secret locks or keys when it comes to conscious evolution.

Accentuating Harmony

Many have the view that life is about constantly giving and sacrificing in order to attain heaven in the afterlife. However, it is not about one-sided unconditional giving in order to receive a reward later on. One's true work serves a dual purpose, providing the function of both giving and receiving at the same time.

"If your compassion does not include yourself it is incomplete."

–Buddha

The idea is that one will reach heaven during the act itself. The reward comes from the experience itself during the work, a gift of life directly from the universe. Soul-purpose makes one feel strong and alive while they do it, but at the same time the individual is providing a service for other's benefit. In this way, one creates harmony on both sides of the spectrum, leading individuals towards freedom and abundance. When people gain from their work on a spiritual level it causes them to feel full on the inside helping them become more giving and generous towards others. These individuals no longer require the consumption of high levels of food or the need to accumulate unnecessary material possessions. At the same time, they provide to others a more passionate and higher quality of work.

Being detached from the giver of life, individuals fall into the world of forms in order to fill their spiritual cavity. Many people work jobs that they do not like, only to use their earnings to purchase possessions that they do not need.[5] As a result, there is disease, sickness, and a lack of abundance in their lives. When the majority of people begin to learn that the conscious experience is malleable and their very well-being, and possibly their position in the afterlife, depends on their conscious evolution in this life, people will place more significance on spiritual growth.

"Set the fire inside desire before they kill your mind."

–Yohei Kawakami

Those that are afraid to follow soul-purpose often look at others who have achieved great heights in the past and come to believe that they cannot become so great. They may be right. However, this is only true for the current version of themselves. The great esoteric knowledge is knowing, and being aware, that the self is evolving and increasing in potential with every new step. With continuing effort, they are activating their spirit and entering into higher dimensions of awareness which afford the ability to step into new possibilities of reality. The individual need only practice until making productive results.

The Conscious Universe

Many lineages around the world, notably Taoism, Buddhism, and Hinduism, insist that each and every being has the entire universe within themselves, and that those who follow the path of truth and self-realization will come to experientially know this truth. When considering that the entire universe is within, as one gradually travels further inward, they are also gaining a deeper connection to the universe outwardly around them. The idea is that by working with one's inner soul, they are also working with the external universe as a whole. The path of becoming "one."

"Coincidence is God's way of remaining anonymous."

–Albert Einstein

A common occurrence while following The Way, and spiraling down the rabbit-hole, is that many people begin to notice strange "coincidences" occurring. Almost like the universe around them is reassuring them and holding their hand.

"The Universe is alive, dead matter cannot create life. We live simultaneously within a super intelligence. It would be foolhardy to assume that the builder of eyes and ears can neither see nor hear. It would also be equally irrational to believe that what gave us the ability of self-awareness is not aware itself."

–Daskalos[6]

If one considers that the universe is alive, then by following truth and by raising one's own consciousness, they are also assisting the larger universe as a whole. By improving themselves they are improving the evolution of mankind as a whole. This is the goal of a Buddhists who use a single candle of enlightenment to light many candles.

> "The Universe is fair and is not equal to everyone.
>
> Only those who deserve get the attention."
>
> –Tian De

Karma, the negative consequences resulting from a negative action is the result of cause and effect. Karma's reach is largely underestimated because of the limited nature of human perception. When one is doing a harmful deed, they are creating a disruption, and that disruption is echoed.

However, the determining factor behind one's good or bad actions is based on feeling more than any accepted set of thought-based "laws." Being internally connected with the external universe, the authenticity an of an evil or destructive act is disclosed through this relationship by feeling. Feeling is the direct result of the connection between an individual and the universe around them, and because of this direct relationship, the ideas that one may conjure in order to justify their actions are much less substantial. The bad feeling that is generated internally is of a deeper nature and due to a connection beyond the local human body/mind.

> "All I can tell you is this, as long as you follow your spirit soul you will be beyond destiny and karmas wretch."
>
> –Tian De

On the opposite side of the spectrum, what is the value of following one's heart? What is the value of doing what one enjoys, that which provokes inner peace? The value is worth more than gold, because it is expanding the quality of one's existence. It is true freedom that is sought after. Karmic Debris is only that which keeps one from connecting with their center, the source of freedom beyond the world. As long as one is not connected with their center (awareness), the individual will never realize their potential and have the capacity to rise experientially beyond karma. The Hindus teach that opening the 6th chakra destroys the karma of previous lives.[7] Whether or not they are beyond karma, an individual at this level is no longer bound mentally and is naturally able to see past illusion and focus their spirit.

"When we are doing the will of our true self, we are inevitably doing the will of the universe. In magic these are seen as indistinguishable. That every human soul is, in fact, the one human soul. It is the soul of the universe itself and as long as you are doing the will of the universe, then it is impossible to do anything wrong."

-Alan Moore[8]

Beyond right and wrong, having knowledge of the self, one becomes able to overcome their past mistakes and clarify their perception. If one knows how to tap into their giver of life, then they will be beyond karma and destiny's wretch. It would follow that doing what makes a person feel alive, is the reason that they are alive.

FREEDOM

A person who is not capable of living with himself is incapable of living with anyone else. One who is not capable of loving himself, enjoying his own company, will not be able to be in deep communion with anyone else.

If you are bored by yourself, you will create boredom in others.

Everyone escapes into a crowd because, to feel the pang of loneliness, is to be afraid; afraid of oneself, afraid of living with oneself. Everyone has done the same thing, so it is a big crowd, and everyone in it is lonely. The crowd is there, but, it is a lonely crowd.

If you are alone, you have freedom. But, when someone else is there, when you are in a crowd, the freedom is lost. Everybody is trying to escape from loneliness. No one wants to be alone and free. One must have company because company means less freedom. To live alone means to choose one life, one self, and one being: the greatest freedom. Only a person who is totally free can surrender, can submit, and can sacrifice their loneliness to be alone.

Only a responsible person can choose wisely.

We are free. We are totally free to choose. Infinitely free to choose whether we want to continue to be born again life after life, birth after birth. Animals are not free. They are conditioned, and in a sense, they are more unconscious. They live by instinct and impulses. They cannot choose because they have a fixed nature and have to follow and abide by it.

Man has no fixed nature. There is no such thing as man's nature or human nature. He has freedom to rise or fall. He can fall lower than the animals or rise higher than the angels. The more expanded his consciousness, the less he is in a bind. Man is totally free to choose.

Freedom has no degree. How can anything with degrees or limitations be called freedom? Freedom means that which is unlimited and has no degrees. Freedom is total. Similarly, there are degrees of hate, but there are no degrees of love. There are degrees of anger but there are no degrees of forgiveness. Either you forgive or you don't. There are degrees in sin, but there are no degrees in virtues.

A lonely person is someone who is empty on the outside from without. And a bored person is someone who is empty inside himself. Boredom is emptiness from within. A lonely and bored person almost always seeks company or companionship from another person who is lonely and bored. Two wrongs cannot make one right.

The body that we have with us now is part of the whole universe. As we are within the entire Universe, the entire Universe is also within us. Because we cannot understand and we conceive it as our own, it has become a problem. If you go deeply within, you will see that the whole universe is a part of you, and you are a part of the universe. Your body is just a part, a constantly changing part of the whole universe. A constant dynamic relationship with the entire whole. Whenever you are, whatever state you are in, you will still be in a body. If your body is taken by the universe, then the universe will give you another body. Unless you become one with the universe. Then there is no need for a body because the universe itself is a body.

A conscious man does not see death as an ignorant man does. Energy is neither created nor destroyed. It just moves from one form to another. Nothing old is ever reborn, and neither does it totally disappear. And that which has once been, will always reappear in a new form. When we say that the soul leaves the body, we mean that it has moved into the Body of the Universe and the universe is constantly giving it another body. This body which you had left behind is still related to you because the whole is related to you as part and parcel of existence in etheric particles. We all leave behind karmic debts, an imprint, an energy, an impression, a shadow and so forth: an aspect that will be dissolved and absorbed into the etheric field of the universe.

Then, according to our karmic imprints and debts, it becomes the blue prints or imprints. With this imprint, a mold is made and it is sent down the production lines through the different processes or departments based on the specifications we have molded, and that is why we have this kind of physical body in this sphere.

The universe will give you another body.

For a man in Consciousness, he will have merged with the universe. A free spirit. Free everywhere. He becomes one who is everywhere and nowhere.

Within our physical body, we have millions of living cells. Every cell within the body has a soul. It's crowded with many living souls as one collective being.
The central Soul is the one that organized, orchestrated, and synthesized everything together. When a cell dies, it merges into the body, and the body will give it another cell body accordingly. Just as we are but one cell in the entire universe whom organized, synthesized each and every one of us as one big community of many souls. We are part of the ocean of life. We can be alone and be free.

-Tian De

THE ETHERIC BODY
[Temple of Clarity]

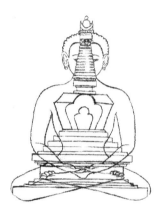

Tibetan Stupa[1] – Thousands erected across all of Tibet, the Stupa statue serves as a visual representation of the etheric body.

"As above so below."

[Hermetic Principle of Correspondence]

When considering the study of human evolution, often times, only shifts of the physical structure are distinguished. For example, this can involve observing physical adaptations in response to adverse environmental conditions. However, these responsive natural modifications to the physical structure of a species take generations to develop. When maintaining a commonplace mindset focused on physical changes, many retain the belief that they do not have the ability to participate in their own evolution. They look at evolution as an involuntary process that reacts for them and over long periods of time. The result of this is that many come to underestimate the importance of exercising their true potential, and instead focus their aim on survival and accumulation.

Nicola Tesla once said,

"The day science begins to study non-physical phenomena it will make more progress in one decade than in all the previous centuries of its existence."

When observing evolution from a non-physical standpoint, one begins to understand that humans have an aspect of themselves that is beyond the physical body, an aspect that can continually grow and intensify. This is the conscious awareness, also known by many ancient cultures as the "spirit." The physical body can be seen as the vessel, and when looking beyond the gross human form, there is the possibility for the evolution of a potential within. Everyone may appear human on the outside, but their current state of evolution can be vastly different, and as such, some are much more advanced than others.

"Your home is your body.
You're the spirit soul staying & living within your physical body.
It's not the outside place that makes you "You."
If you are not happy, that's because you can't identify with
your spirit soul that's pure luminous & free from karma."
−Tian De

Fascinated by experiential evolution, a development that can be equated to reaching God, many ancient philosophers, alchemists, wizards, shaman, gurus, yogis, and priests around the world took initiative towards understanding its deeper mechanics. The fruit of their research revealed that the progression of one's conscious awareness is the development of a subtle nervous system known as the Etheric Body.[2] Throughout the process of "waking up," it is the etheric body that is developing in the background: a framework mapping the development of the spirit-soul, influencing one's health, psychology, and potential.

To a major extent, only certain Asian cultures are predominant at retaining commonplace esoteric knowledge available to the masses: notably Tibet, China, and India. Before the dark ages, however, great alchemical knowledge and understanding was also said to be commonplace in the western world. However, the Inquisition marked a significant loss in knowledge, and as a result, alchemical secrets were carefully hidden, occupying nursery rhymes, fairy tale stories, and folk songs.[3]

When coming across the word alchemy, many think of the pursuit of transforming base metals into gold. This understanding, however, is more of a metaphor. A true alchemist is not interested in creating physical gold. Theoretically they would have no need for it. True alchemy is about transforming the mundane into the spiritual, it is about transforming a normal human into an extraordinary human. Occasionally certain individuals are referred to as a "golden child;" this does not mean that the child is made of gold, but that they have exceptional potential. Alchemy studies why.

The true science of alchemy involves gaining a basic understanding of the "etheric body." This is a part of one's self that represents the development of one's concentration and is connected with the clarity of one's perception: their intimacy with reality.

In order to put the etheric body into proper perspective, one must look at the physical body. What physicists define as "physical" is a representation of matter at a specific range in frequency. When extending the range beyond normal perception, more subtle forms of matter can be observed. As there exist different frequencies of energy, there also exist different frequencies, or layers, of matter. This is the nature of the Etheric Body; an aspect of one's self that is ordinarily beyond human perception. Similar to a dog whistle, which is not perceptible by humans. However, just because we cannot hear the whistle, does not mean that the sound is not being produced. (adapted from Mark Passio).

"If you want to find the secrets of the universe, think in terms of energy, frequency and vibration."

–Nicola Tesla

The etheric body is the energetic counterpart to the physical form, a coexisting body of matter residing on a subtler frequency. As this subtle body is interlayered with the physical body, they are both connected and constantly interacting with each other. With the development of the etheric body comes the development of the physical body. One might notice that some people can be observed constantly glowing with health and vitality. These individuals have developed their etheric body to higher potentials. The glowing phenomenon is the abundance of high frequency vital energy stored in vessels known as "dan tiens" and aureated by the rotating discs known as "chakras."

Structure

While physicists use sophisticated laboratory equipment to study matter, meditators become sensitive to subtle forms of matter ordinarily beyond human perception through awareness-based practices such as meditation. It is through this raised state of awareness that practitioners have become cognizant of the etheric body. Each slightly unique, different groups of people around the world have commonly illustrated the etheric body. The most common and recognized illustrations of the etheric body are the Judaic Tree of Life, Greek Caduceus, Tibetan chakras, Hindu chakras, and the Chinese Daoist Neijing Tu. These illustrations map the alchemical process of converting sexual energy into conscious awareness/intelligence.

The basic framework of the etheric body contains three dan tiens as well as seven major chakras. These two systems are connected and develop naturally in a similar ascending fashion from the base of the spine upwards. As the individual grows consciously, both the chakras and the dan tiens are constantly developing in the background. In the etheric body, the chakras are the amplifiers, and the dan tiens are the batteries.

As the etheric body is activating, or "charging up," one's concentration/awareness increases more and more throwing the individual closer and closer into the present moment; it is the metamorphosis of a normal human being into an extraordinary human being.

The Sacred Disks

The single most significant aspect on the path of conscious evolution is the opening of the sacred disks, also known as the chakras. There exist many chakras, both big and small, throughout the human body; however, the seven major chakras ascending along the spine to the top of the cranium are the main focus of self-transformation: Muladhara, Svadhisthana, Manipura, Anahata, Visuddha, Ajna, and Sahasrara. These chakras are the gates allowing one's sexual energy to rise and manifest as intelligence.

Chakra Illustration[4]

Originating from ancient Sanskrit, some say that the word chakra is literally defined as "wheel," and others will say that it actually means "lock." Either way, both definitions are accurate to a certain extent, because the goal of alchemy is to open each chakra, and when they are open, they begin to spin like a wheel.

Instead of a wheel however, chakras are more closely related to a whirlpool. Whirlpools are large swirling vortexes created in bodies of water by the interaction of two opposing currents. Similarly, chakras are swirling vortexes created by the interaction of two opposing life-force energies. The chakra whirlpools emerge in the body where the channel Ida, the moon/cold apana, converges with the Pingala channel, the solar/warm prana, along the central channel (known as shushumna). The feeling of a vortex erupts from the inside of the individual at the location of a purified chakra. The Chakra is at the point where they meet.

Most widely recognized by a symbol in the medical field, the Greek Caduceus is associated with the Greek god Hermes, known as the messenger of the gods. The Ida and Pingala channels can be seen represented by two snakes. The two snakes cross paths at the point of each chakra and finally converge at the location of the sixth major chakra. Similar to Hindu diagrams, near the sixth chakra there is depicted wings. This is because the head is considered the seat of the soul and the completion of alchemy, that of transmuting sexual energy into intelligence: it is when a person's life takes flight.

Purifying the endocrine system and increasing the potential of the human body results in a resistance to sickness and disease and potentially an increase in the rejuvenation of current injuries at an accelerated rate. This is the forgotten meaning behind the Greek Caduceus and its connection with the medical field.

The Greek Legend of Ophiuchus

The Greek legend of Ophiuchus is centered around a human physician named Asclepius who later became worshipped as a god of medicine. Asclepius was so talented at the art of healing that he was even capable of bringing the dead back to life. However, according to the Greek legend, all of Asclepius's great knowledge and abilities were taught to him from a snake. For this reason, Asclepius is also known as "the serpent bearer." Eventually, Zues, angered by

Asclepius's great knowledge, killed him by striking him with a thunderbolt. This act however immortalized Asclepius and he became painted in the sky as the constellation of Ophiuchus: the less recognized thirteenth member of the Zodiac.[5]

This legend has significant ties with the cultivation of the etheric body, as it is centered around the knowledge of healing being associated with a snake, or more accurately, the control of a snake. Asclepius was, after all, a "snake bearer." Bearing the snake is a metaphor for having mastery over the kundalini energy in the spine: this is attained by awakening the sixth chakra. Bearing the snake is the ability to raise the sexual energy through the sushumna central channel at will. This is the knowledge of healing, because the amplified nervous system as a result of purifying the spine leads to greater health and wellbeing. Also interesting is Asclepius's ability to raise the dead, a similar occurrence associated with masters like Jesus.

Currently, a basic understanding of the etheric body and its importance to health is a major hole in the western medical paradigm. In the future, learning to empower the etheric body will be a major breakthrough in medicine. When western science begins to experimentally become aware of the subtle etheric nervous system, tremendous achievements in health will become possible.

Note: Besides healing, activating the etheric nervous system is also associated with the occurrence of many "supernatural" feats.

Around the world many variations similar to the Greek Caduceus exist, including counterparts with the ancient Sumerians, Aryans, Egyptians, and Celtics. Depending on the origin of the Caduceus, different variations are depicted at the top of the central rod; there can be a flame, a sphere, or a pine cone. The flame represents igniting the mind. The sphere represents the golden "Light of God" and is often connected with the halo. The Celtic Caduceus sometimes is depicted with a hand touching the sphere at the top, which is most commonly understood as touching God. The ancient Sumerian Tree of Life, very similar to the Caduceus, depicts

Sumerian gods placing pine cones at the top. The pine cone is often recognized by many on the Pope's staff and by the giant pine cone statue (known as the Pigna Statue) in the Vatican court yard; it is a representation of the pineal gland. In the brain, the pea-sized pineal gland is roughly the shape of a pine cone. When connecting the chakras with glands, the pineal gland is often associated with the seventh major chakra at the top of the head and is correlated with balancing the right and left hemispheres of the brain. Also, similar to the human eye, the pineal gland has rods and cones which are used as interpreters and transmitters of external information to the brain.[6]

2 Tibetan Chakra Image

Rivaling the Indian Kundalini diagrams, the Tibetan diagram is probably the most practical of all depictions of the etheric body known today. One might notice that there are more than seven chakras ascending the spine. This is a more accurate representation, as the seven are known as "major" because there also exist minor chakras along the spine. Therefore, during meditation practice or training, one will most likely feel more than seven chakras moving up the spine. The flower is the most accurate representation of the etheric body at the top of the head. Also, when looking at the Tibetan Chakra diagram, the kundalini snake starts at the third chakra. This is very accurate because when the third chakra is activated that is when the kundalini snake becomes awakened. This is when the lower dan tien, the source of sexual power, is activated. Outside of the body in the diagram, the background is divided into three sections. These sections represent an individual's level of conscious awareness as they ascend the spine, correlating with Hell, Earth, and Heaven.

Tree of Life Diagram

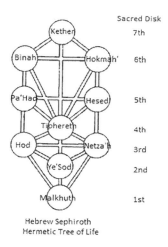

Sacred Disk
7th
6th
5th
4th
3rd
2nd
1st

Hebrew Sephiroth
Hermetic Tree of Life

Each sepheroth/chakra represents a center of knowledge and understanding. In this diagram, some are dual, which means that they have preserving or destructive characteristics.

Chakras are literally a map or a key to the process of human development: upgrading the clarity and depth of one's existence. Because of the expanding quality of this process, each chakra that opens can comparatively be seen as unlocking a different dimension of reality for the individual. During this process an individual's complete life view can change, it is not like some diet plan, and is more like taking the red pill from the Wachowki Brother's film The Matrix.

Many of these diagrams are accompanied by training practices aimed towards purifying and activating the etheric nervous system to higher potentials, leading to conscious expansion and more "control" of one's existence. A few of the related practices are Daoist Alchemy, Kundalini Yoga, Western Hermetics, Esoteric Judaism, Egyptian Yoga, and Tibetan Tantra/Meditation.

Correlations: Christianity/Muslim

Besides the major chakras being visually depicted in the different diagrams above, they also have made appearances in Islam and Christianity. In Islam, the chakras are symbolically referred to as the "Seven Heavens to Allah". The seven heavens of Allah are "stages" that one must go through in order to reach the god Allah. This is most likely referring to the seven chakras, or stages of awareness, leading one to more concentrated levels of experiential consciousness.

Revelation 4:1-8:1 / A Scroll (wisdom) sealed with seven seals.[8]

The chakras connection to Christianity is best depicted by the "Seven Seals" on the scroll of wisdom described in Revelation 5 to 1. The "Seven Seals" described in the Book of Revelation are seven symbolic seals that keep the scroll of wisdom closed and secure.

As the seven seals are a representation for the seven chakras of an individual, opening the seals one-by-one is a symbolic representation of opening the seven major chakras along the spine. This process is referred to in Revelation as an "apocalypse." However, the word apocalypse does not mean the end of the outer world, but instead it is referring to the destruction of one's ignorance. Translated literally from ancient Greek, apokalupto, the word apocalypse means a disclosure of knowledge, or "an uncovering," "a lifting of the veil." In alchemy, after the kundalini has been awakened people are never the same, it is a metamorphic process, whereby the inner world of the individual is transformed and purified profoundly. The "scroll" represents true wisdom, that which is only obtained by having a purified experiential perception. When the scroll is opened (centers 1-7), the mind of the individual is opened as well. This is the lifting of the veil and the disclosure of truth. When the inner world of an individual is transformed, the outer world is unveiled.

The opening of the seven seals on this "apocalyptic" scroll occurs in Revelation Chapters 5-8. When looking at 8:1, the opening of the seventh seal is described as the most significant, with the occurrence of bringing silence. The opening of the seventh seal is the opening of the seventh major chakra, and the silence described is mental silence.

The Three Dan Tiens

One commonality between the observations of scientists and meditators with regards to subtle matter is quantum mechanics. Quantum mechanics verifies from a scientific standpoint that subtle matter behaves as both a particle and as a wave (Double-Slit Experiment). Similarly, the subtle life-force energy known as chi or prana also exists as both a particle and as a wave/liquid. Chi exists in the air as a particle, often described in Hermetic sciences as a seven-colored vitality globule,[9] but throughout the body, it behaves as a liquid. Often illustrated by acupuncture diagrams, chi flows in the state of a liquid through each of an individual's meridians, defined as "rivers of energy."

When looking at the accumulation of life-force energy in the etheric body, the three Dan Tiens serve as storage containers for the different frequencies/consistencies. The three primary dan tiens within the etheric body in Daoist Alchemy are the Lower Dan Tien, Middle Dan Tien, and Upper Dan Tien. Within the etheric body these three major dan tiens serve as storage containers, holding the vital energy that humans absorb from their surroundings. The dan tien system is the battery or power source of the etheric body.

These vital energies, or fluids, are primarily obtained through the food one eats, the air one breaths, direct contact with the earth (yin chi absorption at Hui Yin point near perineum), and also directly from the sun itself (yang chi absorption at Ba Hui point at the top of head). One method that practitioners use to find the Ba Hui point is by touching the top of one's ears with their thumbs and then touching the middle fingers together at the top of the head where it feels energetically active. I believe that the Ba Hui point can also be found at a cross section of the skull known as the Anterior Fontanelle, between the frontal bone and parietal bone.

Each of the three dan tiens houses a different frequency/consistency of vital energy. Because of their influence over the physical body, ancient Daoists referred to them as the "three elixirs," or the "three medicines." As a person develops consciously they are absorbing and refining these three vital energies creating health in the physical body and eventually luminosity. Because the vital energy serves as a medicine for the physical body, the capacity of an individual's dan tien system strongly influences their overall health and well-being; the capacity of each dan tien in an individual can even be estimated visually by different characteristics of an individual's physical body.

The three elixirs accumulate in the body like the structure of a pyramid. The first elixir, known as jing, accumulates in the lowest dan tien, but then jing is continually refined and raised to fill the middle dan tien. The middle dan tien houses chi. The chi housed in the middle dan tien is further refined into shen which accumulates in the upper dan tien.

Spiritually connected individuals may not be growing additional limbs, but the physical body also goes through a noticeable metamorphosis. The human body, a form of gross matter, slowly shifts and carves itself to higher degrees of perfection along with the inner development of the awareness: attaining a level of vibrancy, intelligence, and potentially perfect health.

下丹田
Lower Dan Tien - Jing [Vitality]

The lowest dan tien, often referred to as the foundation, is the largest container and holds the vital energy jing. Jing is the most unrefined of the three treasures and has the least luminosity. Jing is the gross form of energy that has been directly absorbed at the Bai Hui point at the top of the head from the sun. It is this continual influx of jing that causes the top of the head to always be warm. When the awareness has been developed, jing can be felt as thick and warm. Jing is often equated with one's essence, with the capacity of the lower dan tien being attributed to one's physical vitality: reflected by the state of the physical body. The level of one's jing is commonly found by observing the health of one's teeth. For this reason, in ancient times, slaves being carried by ships would be judged by the condition of their teeth as a measurement for looking at the condition of the physical body as a whole.

As the lower dan tien houses sexual energy, it also functions as the "golden stove" for the alchemical process of transmuting sexual energy into intelligence. When compared with a car, the lower dantien serves as the engine.

中丹田
Middle Dan Tien - Chi [Energy]

Housed in the middle dan tien is the vital energy known as Chi. Chi is more refined than jing and is also slightly luminous with no discernable temperature.

Where jing is known as vitality, Chi is known as energy. The accumulation of chi is responsible for the daily energy that an individual has available during their waking hours. Chi is reflected in the physical body by the glowing of the skin, causing the body to appear slightly luminous. Because of this, these people usually come across others to as very attractive. After being cultivated sufficiently, heat will begin to be felt in the middle dan tien (chest area). When compared with a car, chi would be like the gasoline in a car.

上丹田
Upper Dan Tien - Shen [Spirit]

The third elixir, known as Shen, is housed in the upper dan tien near the center of the cranium. The upper dan tien is the smallest in size, and therefore holds the least capacity. Shen, however, is the most refined, and also the most luminous of the three elixirs. When the third dan tien is filled with shen, the field of light around the head will be complete: sometimes referred to as the globe of shen, or as simply the "halo" of golden light.

The golden light is a representation of profound levels of concentration. When entering concentration, the sexual energy within the body is continually refined until reaching a frequency to that of golden light (Shen). The individual accumulating Shen is actually becoming more illuminated, or "brighter:" a common way people often refer to those with extraordinary intelligence. However, as the illumination is originating from a subtle "non-physical" substance, the golden light of the halo is not ordinarily perceived from conscious standpoint.

Note: The term "physical" is a perceivable range of matter, and is not an absolute condition. As all matter is energy residing at different frequencies, the term non-physical refers to matter outside of normal human perception.

When looking at the human body, the human spirit, the cultivation of shen, is reflected by the glowing of the eyes. Returning to the car analogy, accumulating shen is like putting a professional race car driver in the car. These individuals have the focus necessary to overcome the most difficult of obstacles and create their dreams into a reality.

Considering that conscious evolution is a natural process, through-out human history, across different areas of the world, one can find illustrations of individuals who have cultivated the halo (field of shen). A few of the most well-known illuminated beings in human history include Jesus, Buddha, Shiva, Guan Yin, Padmasambhava, and Krishna.

Illustrations: Jesus[10], Buddha,[11] Shiva,[12] Petroglyph[13]

The halo phenomenon is also depicted in ancient petroglyphs in different parts of the world. Besides the image above from Valle Camonica, Italy, the Vantage Petroglyph[14] in Washington, USA is also notable. These ancient petroglyphs, however, are often grouped in the "Ancient Astronaut Hypothesis," because the circle depicted around the head somewhat resembles the modern astronaut helmet. The astronaut theory, however, does not account for the lines often drawn coming out of the circle. These lines are depicting a shining effect from the halo, similar to the Buddha image above.

Because of its outward nature, the halo is the single most common attribute connected with spiritually illuminated beings throughout history. These individuals were human at one point and were born on Earth, but through following inner-truth and self-refinement they were able to transcend the ordinary human condition.

While many view Jesus as the Son of God, the monks of eastern Christianity, notably in Greece, will often teach a different perspective with regard to Jesus Christ: pointing out that he was not "the" Son of God, but he was instead "a" Son of God.[15] This is an important distinction that emphasizes we are all Sons of God and have the capacity to achieve what Jesus did. Through the process of self-refinement, Jesus Christ was able to attain a state of consciousness that is more directly connected with the universe around him: he was reborn into the "The Kingdom of God."

The development of shen is connected with an alteration of perception: an awakening experience that transcends one's ordinary human nature. Where jing deals with physical health, and chi with daily energy, shen deals with spirit/intensity/awareness. The halo of shen that is created alters an individual's relation to their mind and body.

While the halo is historically regarded as a symbol of mastery and transcendence, it also serves a very functional purpose.

From a physical perspective, the attainment of shen can be seen as directly stimulating the brain: notably the pineal gland, responsible for altering one's conscious perception. From an alchemical perspective, the golden light of the halo creates a protective field that keeps the mind clear of thought-forms. This protective field prevents one from becoming lost in thoughts, and allows the awareness to be eternally sustained. Many have probably heard the phrase about the "mind being clouded." Shen is a light illuminating from the center of one's head, clearing away any mental clouding and placing the individual in direct contact with every moment. It is uncontrollable thoughts which displace an individual and cause them to leave the present moment. Because of this constant state of uncontrollable displacement, many ordinary people are considered by alchemists to be "asleep" in their waking lives: detached from self-realization.

Note: In the field of neurotheology, the study of neural correlations of religion and spirituality, there have been efforts to technologically replicate the functionality of the halo. Notably, the Koren Helmet, also known as the "God Helmet," developed by Stanley Koren and Michael Persinger. While criticized, Persinger reported many of the subjects using the helmet experienced mystical phenomenon and altered states.[16] The helmet uses magnetic fields targeted at specific points in the brain, similar to yoga, which raises the apana (magnetic) energy to the brain. As of today, while I have not had any personal experience with the helmet, after some research I believe that the device certainly works to a limited extent.

Cultivation

Every child begins with substance in the three dan tiens, but with time most individuals lose sight of self-refinement as they age and begin to unconsciously develop backwards. Initially losing shen (upper dan tien) to supply chi (middle dan tien), and finally losing chi to supply jing (lower dan tien). The purpose of alchemy, therefore, is to refill the dan tiens, starting with the foundation, and activate one's spirit. As the "three elixirs" are also a determining factor of the overall health and radiance of the physical body, the purpose of Daoist longevity arts is to restore them and offset the aging process.

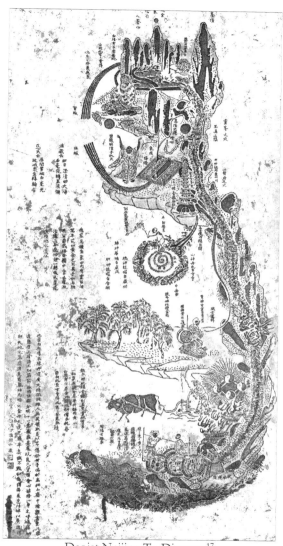

Daoist Neijing Tu Diagram[17]

73

The Daoist Neijing Tu

The Neijing Tu is the Chinese Daoist "inner landscape" diagram, serving as a diagram of internal cultivation associated with meditation arts (Neidan). The Neijing Tu is a depiction of the human body as a microcosm of nature; an inner landscape.[1] At first glance, the diagram appears like a map for ascending a mountain. However, in actuality, it is more of a metaphor depicting the alchemical process of climbing one's own inner mountain towards truth.

All known copies of the Neijing Tu originate from an engraved stele dated 1886 in Beijing's White Cloud Temple. However, the age of the diagram itself is unknown because the stele records how it is based on an ancient silk scroll recovered by Liu Chengyin on Mount Song.[2]

Because the diagram in the White Cloud Temple is engraved in stone, copies of the diagram are often referred to as "rubs," connoting the rubbing method used to copy the diagram.

The Neijing Tu is the Chinese visual representation of the etheric body and the process of inner alchemy: that of transmuting sexual energy (jing) into intelligence. The Neijing Tu illustration represents the side-view of a person. The trees near the middle of the diagram correspond with where the human liver is. On the right side of the diagram, the river flowing up from the base all the way to the top of the head is a representation of the sexual energy flowing up the central channel known as sushumna. In the diagram, the river originates from a large body of water at the base, known as the lower dan tien, and then it is carried up the spine and eventually to the top of the head, known as the crown center in other systems.

At the base of the diagram, a boy and a girl are working a water wheel that moves the water up the spine. This is a representation of the function of the lower dan tien. The boy represents yang and the girl is yin, similar to the Ida and Pingala; they help the river flow up the sushumna central channel. In alchemy, when the lower dan tien is activated, the kundalini becomes awakened and the sexual energy (jing) is able to rise up the spine. The illustration of the water wheel also makes the important distinction that the lower dan tien is the power source behind the kundalini (sexual energy) that rises up the spine.

While the sexual energy is ascending the Sushumna channel in the spine, the energy will need to pass through the three hindrances, referred to in Daoist alchemy as "the three gates." In Daoist lore, these gates are said to be imposed on humans by the gods because of their sins as a measure to separate humans from their true potential.[3] The first gate is located near the tailbone, the second at the shoulder blades, and the third is at the base of the skull. The gates are illustrated on the legendary Neijing Tu diagram, however, they are difficult to see. The first gate is the largest and can easily be seen to the right of the boy and girl working the waterwheel. The three gates prevent the sexual energy from raising to new plateaus, preventing the dantiens from being fully cultivated. While the gates serve as hindrances for the kundalini energy, they are not anything of concern and will open of their own accord when the practitioner is ready.

The Neijing Tu is a fascinating diagram, and for those that would like to delve deeper with respect to each aspect of the diagram, I recommend reading *Nei-Ching T'u: Diagram of the Inner Channels*.

Looking at the Chakras and Dan Tiens

Naturally, the dan tien system and the chakra system develop in tandem from the bottom of the spine up to the top of the head. The three major dan tiens work hand-in-hand with the chakra system. The dan tiens are the batteries, and the chakras are the amplifiers. The dan tiens supply the power in the form of vital energy to the chakras. Therefore, the amount of vital energy accumulated in the dan tiens, notably the lower dan tien, determines the power of concentration available at each chakra, thus providing the power behind the practitioner's ability to concentrate.

Because it is an interconnected system, both the chakras and the dan tiens play an important role in conscious development, and therefore should both be integrated in any form of technique based system. Those who follow the path of natural evolution or awareness-based meditation are naturally cultivating both systems in harmony. The practitioner will be both absorbing vital energy and also refining their concentration to higher levels.

Analyzing the Sacred Disks

The chakras are layers of concentration; with each new awakening the individual reaches a new level of concentration. The spine, specifically the sushumna channel, is the dimension of an individual that determines which direction they go in life. If one perceives life from the higher chakras, then the same situation will be different for them than if they perceived life from the lower chakras.[4]

The lower three chakras are connected with preserving the body: they represent self-preservation and survival. The heart chakra is often illustrated by the combination of two opposite triangles. This is because the heart chakra is the middle grounds for the upper and lower three chakras. The upper three chakras represent the head and the heart, they encourage one to go beyond; to go beyond what is ordinary.[5]

General Overview of Chakras

Kundalini

Kundalini is the sexual energy that is raised up through the chakras one by one as a result of regular concentration. Because of its nature, the kundalini is often compared with a coiled snake. The Hindi word "kundala" translates to "coiled." The kundalini energy, is the sexual energy that is "coiled" or dormant in the lower dan tien, but that once awakened rises up like a snake, higher and higher, as each chakra is purified.

"When the Kundalini ascends one Chakra or Yogic center, the Yogi also ascends one step or rung upward in the Yogic ladder; one more page, the next page, he reads in the divine book; the more the Kundalini travels upwards, the Yogi also advances towards the goal or spiritual perfection in relation to it."

–Swami Sivananda[6]

As illustrated by the Neijing Tu, purifying the central channel can be compared with climbing up a mountain. For those who regularly concentrate, the chakras naturally open from the base of the spine upwards to the top of the head. The higher up the chakras that the kundalini rises, the more intense the reality.

When one engages in concentration/meditation, they awaken and lift their kundalini, a powerful energy that can be felt. When confronted with a dormant chakra, overtime, the kundalini purifies, awakens, and activates it. The chakras are referred to as "knots" by the Tibetans because when they are dormant they do not allow the sexual energy to rise up the sushumna channel. Once a chakra is purified/opened, the sexual energy (jing/kundalini) is able to travel higher up the central sushumna channel in the spine.

The kundalini acts as a power cord that connects the power source (lower dan tien) with the amplifier (chakra). The goal in alchemy/yoga is to connect the power source (lower dan tien) with the sixth chakra in the brain. By doing this, one connects their sexual energy with the center of concentration, amplifying their existence. At the sixth chakra one becomes a true alchemist, able to convert sexual energy into spirit, or shen. By connecting the power source with the spirit/intelligence: a mundane individual becomes extraordinary. Historically, this is sometimes known as obtaining the "rod of power," because when this occurs the individual gains mastery/control over the kundalini. Awareness beyond mind.

Sushumna refers to having the quality of no color but also having all colors. It is the tendency of those who awaken the sushumna central channel to have no prejudice and not reject the flow of life. It is a transparent quality associated with wisdom. It is said that where ever they go, they also become, but nothing sticks to them.[7] It is realization past duality that can see the good and bad in each choice or decision.

Some alchemical systems work with the higher chakras directly, with the goal of tapping into a higher state of awareness at an accelerated pace. An example of this would be to repeatedly use mantras like AUM and flame concentration techniques in order to activate and open the 6th chakra directly. The problem with this approach, is that the major energy centers below the 6th are not awakened, so there will not be an open channel (Sushumna Nadi) through which to provide power to the 6th chakra. For this reason, many people can practice the higher level techniques for long periods of time and not make adequate progress, because the higher chakra is not connected to the power source (lower dan tien). If they do awaken the higher chakras, over time, it will easily become dormant again because it is not connected to the kundalini energy, and one will slowly lose all of their hard work. Using higher level techniques too soon is almost like jumpstarting a car with no gas. The techniques are not worthless, but they should be supplemented with training that cultivates one's foundation (meditation/soul-purpose).

However, acting the etheric body is a purification process. One could say that when each new chakra is activated, certain amounts of "karmic debris" are released. This can sometimes lead a person to experience certain levels of instability including shifts in behavior and emotions—some refer to this as "Kundalini Sickness." Personally, however, I believe that such concerns should be disregarded.

Activating the Etheric Body
Sacred Disk Purification

As one's awareness expands through alchemical practices, the practitioner gradually becomes more and more familiar with both the subtle energies surrounding them and with the etheric body itself. During the activation of the first three chakras, the sensations produced are very minute and nearly non-existent. Many who try meditation do not get past the stage of awakening these initial centers and eventually give up their practice. However, with time and continual training, (fourth chakra and up), the sensations become more pronounced.

While climbing this ladder of awareness, each chakra has three primary stages of development: Pulsing, Activation, and Open.

Pulsing – The chakra is just developing and giving off a pulsing sensation. At this stage, the chakra is gathering energy.

Activation (spinning) – The activation phase is when the chakra has actually begun to spin and is rotating like a wheel. For higher chakras, the activation phase is accompanied with vibration sensations created from the spinning. At this stage, through conscious awareness, the practitioner can make the chakra spin at a faster and faster rate, leading to a purification of the chakra. When the chakra is spinning easily, it will spin faster and then slow down, faster and then slow down; speeding up on each repetition. Often times, during this process, one will begin to see a blur when their eyes are closed, and by centering and focusing on this blur, the chakra will be developed directly. Eventually, with the later chakras (6th chakra and up), the blur can become very bright as a result of the chakra speeding up.

Note: During the activation phase of the higher chakras, it is possible that the sleep cycle of the individual will begin changing as well. This is because when a chakra is newly activated, it begins to introduce a higher level of amplification to the current nervous structure. As a result, for a short time, the nervous system is exposed to more than it is normally used to, leading to more wakefulness and an alteration to the sleep cycle. Eventually the nervous system adjusts naturally.

Open – Working with the chakras is like starting an old prop-plane, they have to reach a certain speed in order to open. Until this point has been reached, the chakra will not be open, but only at a certain stage of activation. During the activation stage, the chakra is spinning, and through continual practice, it will spin easier, and easier, until the chakra is finally open. With the higher chakras, usually the fourth chakra and above, until it is fully open, one may see light in their mind's eye that becomes brighter and brighter as the chakra develops. This light can be utilized as a tool for concentration.

Continuous Progression is the Key

It is important to train daily; each phase of chakra awakening is like a flower blooming. The seed stage, growing, and then eventually blooming.

If an individual is solely training alchemical methods then they should make time so that they can be training at least a 90 minutes each day, consisting of two 45 minute intervals. For some, if the individual is consistent with their training, each chakra can take around two to four months to open. Ultimately, understanding the chakras and their development is interesting, but it is important to remain detached as to where one thinks they are in their development; the less one expects the better.

Activation Experiences

During the activation phase of the major chakras, individuals can have strange experiences during the night while sleeping or especially while napping in the day time. This can be associated to some degree with what many refer to as sleep paralysis. Sometimes these experiences can even be terrifying to some degree. However, they are harmless and more of a sign that one is progressing.

Sacred Disc Awakening Descriptions

"This whole universe rests in Thy bosom. Crores of salutations unto thee. O Mother of this world! Lead me on to open the Sushumna Nadi and take Thee along the Chakras to Sahasrara Chakra and to merge myself in Thee and Thy consort, Lord Siva. Kundalini Yoga is that Yoga which treats of Kundalini Sakti, the six centres of spiritual energy (Shat Chakras), the arousing of the sleeping Kundalini Sakti and its union with Lord Siva in Sahasrara Chakra, at the crown of the head."

–Swami Sivananda[1]

Volumes of yogic texts have gone into detail about the specific attributes associated with each major chakra. However, the attributes are not very important to the serious practitioner. What is more important is to gradually move forward, working towards continually amplifying one's existence. Becoming fixated upon the sensations and/or expecting future sensations from each chakra causes individuals to stagnate and halt their progression.

Below are a few of the important details and sensations associated with each chakra so as to give the serious practitioner a better understanding of the process of purifying the etheric body.

Chakras One, Two, and Three:

The sensations and experiences associated with the first three chakras can be summed up together because the occurrences caused by working with the first three chakras are very subtle. This is partially because at this stage the individual has the least amount of concentration and awareness. Their awareness is still "physical." Many begin training and quickly give up after only a few weeks with no noticeable results, coming to believe the etheric body is fiction.

Opening the third chakra is associated with will power. During this point of my training, I started attempting ambitious training techniques like water fasting for five days. I have met a few people who can go for a month without problems, but it was very difficult for me because I did not prepare for it. I would not recommend fasting or any other form of training that is too harsh. The health and well-being of the physical body is much more important, and consistent practice is key.

A very important aspect regarding opening the third major chakra is that it activates the lower dan tien, thus awakening the kundalini. At this stage, one may begin to notice slight sensations such as heat near the navel when doing deep breathing exercises.

Chakra Four:

When the practitioner activates the heart chakra, truly noticeable sensations begin to be felt. When the heart chakra begins to activate, one may experience a strong sensation of electricity throughout the body during meditation. This only lasts a few days and will most likely stop completely as the body adjusts.

When the heart chakra finally opens, it is the first real profound experiential occurrence. For the first day, a slight shift in one's state of being can be very noticeable, but then the individual quickly becomes accustomed to it. At this stage a person's entire life view can change dramatically. One can begin to develop an urge to follow truth and "follow their heart." The time surrounding the period of opening the heart chakra is also often accompanied with powerful emotional fluctuations.

As the heart chakra, represented by two opposing triangles, is the meeting grounds between one's desire for self-preservation and the desire/longing to go beyond, the experience of opening it creates the likelihood of one following a path to go beyond.

When this experience occurred for me, I was studying Finance at the time in London. I woke up and went outside feeling a certain high. The following days I cried for the first time in many years because of an emotional pain that I had felt inside. At this time, I also dropped out of school, because I was not actually fascinated with what I was studying at the time.

Accompanying the opening of the heart chakra is also the ability to see the first layer of the aura in others. This is the etheric body permeating around the physical body. This layer of the aura is clear, but because of the reflection from sunlight, it often appears blue or yellow.

At this point, the meditator will actually be able to feel each of the individual chakras to some extent. However, the practitioner still does not have control over the sensations or the chakras, so the occurrences are mostly random.

During meditation one still does not have control of the kundalini at this point either, so meditations are not perfect and the individual still gets lost in thought. At this time, during in my meditations, I was occasionally seeing a blue blur that I would occasionally concentrate on.

Chakra Five:

The throat chakra represents the fifth element aether in yogic/Tibetan studies. The enigmatic nature of this element, connects closely to the nature of this chakra. The activation of the fifth chakra does not bring many profound experiences. At the time, I myself was not even aware that I had opened it. It is difficult to tell how developed it is, and because of this, it makes opening the sixth chakra a surprise.

At this stage, the individual's concentration increases further, allowing them to have a better degree of awareness during meditation practice. One can rest in awareness for longer and longer periods of time while the thoughts pass by.

At this level the practitioner will still not have control of their chakra system. However, they will have experiences that remind them that they are on the right track. It is very likely at this stage that one is able to focus their awareness on individual chakras and cause them to activate. The sensation of vibrations during meditation also expands wider, becoming slightly felt even outside of the body.

After the fifth chakra is fully developed, one of the signs that the practitioner is close to activating the sixth chakra is that they will feel heat in their chest. This heat is from the middle dantien being fully cultivated and ready to transform into shen. However, in order for this to occur, the "third gate," as it is referred to in Daoism needs to open and allow the sexual energy to reach the sixth chakra. Only by going "through the gate" and by reaching the sixth chakra is the kundalini sexual energy able to transmute into shen.

Opening the fifth chakra is like lowering a bridge, allowing the kundalini energy in the body to reach the head. At this stage of development, practitioners can slightly tuck in their neck while practicing meditation so as to open the flow of energy into the head. This is in order to assist with opening the sixth chakra. The Indian yogis also have their own unique technique for creating this energy bridge called Jalandhara Bandha, which can be practiced separately for short intervals of time. However, it is not necessary.

Development of the Etheric Body[2] - Opening the Sixth Sacred Disc

Opening the sixth chakra marks the entrance to sagehood. This is the goal of alchemy, the stage of transmuting sexual energy into spirit. It is the evolution of a soul into a spirit, a destruction of the mundane—in some traditions, an achievement akin to becoming an immortal.

From an alchemical perspective, opening the sixth chakra is the achievement of Natural Fusion. On a kundalini diagram, the fusion at the sixth chakra is represented by the heads of two serpents joining together. At this point, the yin and yang energies fuse together. This fusion is both the purpose and goal of yoga. Yoga was originally known as Yog, but because of the British accent, it became popularly known as "yoga." In Hindi, the word yog means union—a direct reference to the sixth chakra fusion. The union is a reference to the yin and yang or prana and apana energies combining at the sixth chakra. Also, in India, the symbol for yoga is the Seal of Solomon. Sol-o-Mon is referring to the Sun and Moon being combined, which refers to the masculine and feminine energies fusing together.

When the sixth chakra opens it is an important evolutionary occurrence known as "Seeing the Light." During its opening, the individual sees a very bright white light as a result of the electric (solar) energy and the magnetic (moon) energy combining inside the head. The light (electromagnetic) that is seen is actually real.

At this stage in my training I was doing on and off half-lotus/full-lotus meditation, sitting for one to two hours without moving. On the side, I was also occasionally practicing the sixth chakra flame meditation technique.[3] At this stage, during meditation, after practicing for an hour without moving, I began to focus on a vague blur that would go away and then reappear. Eventually, one day it became brighter and brighter; it became focused and then suddenly flashed brighter than the sun. After that, the bright light was gone, but my meditations changed forever. This experience was the opening of the sixth chakra.

There were no activation or pulsing signs or sensations beforehand to let me know that I was close to achieving fusion. However, I had enough awareness to at least know that I was cultivating the fifth or sixth chakra. The most recent sensation at the time, before fusion, was a strong feeling of heat in the chest—a sensation associated with fully developing the middle dan tien, and a sign that the third Daoist gate is ready to open.

An individual who has reached this stage is sometimes referred to as a master, because at this point one develops concentration beyond the mind, gaining control of the kundalini serpent. They can raise the kundalini at will and enter into deep states of concentration. This level of concentration gives the individual control over their kundalini allowing them to enter true focused meditation at will.

Not until the sixth chakra is open will a person become truly familiar with and gain a degree of mastery over the chakra system. Until fusion is attained, the sensations and experiences related to kundalini are uncontrollable by the individual. They can feel the chakras, but they can connect consciously raise the kundalini at will. This is known as having the "rod of power," and at this stage the meditation experience becomes truly profound. The previous meditation training was aimed towards having awareness unobstructed by the mind, but at this stage, the quote "in stillness there is movement" begins to apply, because the individual can concentrate directly on what they see in their mind's eye. They will feel the kundalini rising and then geometric figures/shapes will begin to appear that they can concentrate on one-pointedly without interruption.

On a side note, it is fascinating to me that one can see perfect geometric figures when closing their eyes. They are mathematical shapes that one would think wer invented by man, yet they are embedded in our consciousness.

Also, after awakening the sixth chakra, the experience of dreams shifts—dreaming becomes more vivid, almost movie-like.

Non-Physical Awareness

After fusion, one becomes aware of yin chi. Following this, the individual's awareness with regards to the non-physical becomes external. They are sensitive to their own and others' etheric body, allowing for the possibility of clearing blockages. To a certain extent, the individual's imagination also becomes external—the forms they think of and create can now be experientially felt. During meditation, the individual can also feel the aura around their body, allowing for the possibility of feeling small ghosts and other non-physical entities.

Another interesting sensation is that when the sixth chakra is open, the third eye also slightly opens. At first this can be felt like a subtle eye on the forehead, giving the individual enhanced awareness of psychic phenomenon. However, with more development, the eye later begins to feel completely physical, but the sensation of its existence continues to appear and disappear.

Nine Chambers of the Upper Dan Tien

Between the sixth and seventh major chakras there are an estimated nine miniature chakras. However, considering the potency of the individual's meditation at this stage, these energy centers open quickly and are not significant.

Chakra Seven - [The Crown]

The key characteristic of the seventh chakra is the opening of the mind on both a subtle level and experientially. This stage represents the birth of the creator, because the individual's creativity flourishes. The activation of the seventh sacred disc at the top of the head combines the left-brain logical hemisphere with the right-brain creative hemisphere. One has both the idea and the initiative required to bring their creations into existence.

CREATION

Be a co-creator.

To be co-creator means you co-exist with the creator.

Everything is already created for us.

A co-creator uses it creatively.

A sculptor cuts and shapes the stone into forms inspired by his creative spark.

He did not create the stone, he used the created stone creatively.

Co-creation means to bring heaven on earth.

Co-creation is not just for sculptors, musicians, artists...

It includes mineral, aquatic, plant, animal and human kingdoms.

We are all creatures of creation.

We need to deal with all these Creatures creatively.

Creation comes from the creator.

We are the Created.

The created comes from the Creator.

And since we are created by the creator, we have the creative quality in us.

To reach the creator, we need to use that creative spark within us.

Then you can use this creative quality to co-create with the creation.

The more you co-create, the more you will understand creation.

And the more you understand creation, the closer you get to the
Creator.

Every creature is his creation.

We are all part and parcel of creation.

All of us are not called creatures if we are not created.

And if you can see everything is part and parcel of the creator, and
you treat them with awe and respect, then you cease to be created.

You will be given the throne of the creator as co-creator.

In actual fact, The Creator does not need to create. It is the co-
creator's work.

And we must work to understand so that we can qualify ourselves to
sit in that throne as His ambassador of creation.

If you love the Creator, loves His creation, created creatures.

-Tian De

Stepping into the creative position is an evolutionary
expression that those who have awakened the seventh sacred disk
begin to do naturally. These individuals have an open mind and begin
to look at reality from a different perspective—that of observing the
created. Many people will explain how they are just not creative,
however, I would argue that creativity is the quality of an evolved
mind. When clarity is developed, the individual no longer feels
attachments towards the belief systems of others. As a result, they
begin to believe in their own ability and come to harness the creative
potential within themselves.

The activation of the seventh chakra also opens the mind
on a subtle level. At this stage, the individual is "crowned creator."
The origins of this title can be understood by the actual sensation on

the top of the head that accompanies the awakening of the seventh disc. On an etheric level, the top of the head actually blooms open like a lotus flower. They are literally "open-minded." The occurrence of the blooming of the top of the head like a flower is illustrated in the Tibetan Etheric Body image. This occurrence is actually very reminiscent of going "super saiyan" in the show *Dragon Ball Z* by Funimation Studios. However, etheric level developments are usually only perceptible by those who meditate and are sensitive to their subtle body. Once a yogi feels their head bloom open, it is no longer a possibility and is instead a reality.

For many, it might sound completely absurd that a highly evolved intellectual being is characterized from an etheric perspective as having a blooming flower on the top of their head. What similarity do humans have to flowers? However, if one really observes the human body, they will find that humans are actually very similar in structure to a plant. One of the best examples is by looking at the human nervous system. The museum exhibit "Body Worlds" has taken the human nervous system and actually modeled it very clearly—this can be freely by searching Google Images. This exhibit clearly shows that the nature of the human nervous system, spine, and brain are very similar to a plant. Personally, I believe it is from this understanding that Western Hermetic alchemists refer to the chakras along the spine as, "The Tree of Life."

Lastly, with the awakening of the seventh chakra one will also feel the fountain of youth sensation; this is the sensation of drops of liquid flowing down the body.

Why Creativity?

Being a creator is the natural quality of an evolved being, a more fully developed intelligence. Why do those who have evolved to the seventh center, and beyond, spend their time in the creative state?

Meditate = Me Dictate

One aspect has to do with the individual's state of mind during the creative process. From a developmental point of view, creating is a method for self-refinement, requiring prolonged periods of increased levels of concentration and self-control—traits that develop an individual's potential. In the creative process, the creator exercises control both internally and externally, requiring a level of concentration that increases one's ability to "see": true dharma. It is the creative process that sets an individual out of ordinary replicated belief systems (that which contain/cloud the mind) and encourages them into an expressive, concentration-based mental state. During meditation practice the individual is being aware of when they thinking, and not simply being consumed by their thoughts. Similarly, in the creative process, the individual is observing each thought with awareness and formulating them consciously. The creative process can be practice that develops mastery of the mind, but it is also the natural product one's mastery of the mind.

Through creation the individual is working towards becoming free both materially and mentally. Instead of spending time serving a function, the individual is consistently working on new creations to serve functions in his/her place. This is like exponentially increasing one's productivity. From this perspective, creating is the ultimate path to flourishing. Being the creator, the individual is also working towards sustaining control of their mind, and attaining mental freedom. Those who are creating are unbounded with regards to concentration as they are constantly in a mind-state of operating faster and faster without any system in place to restrain them. When one eventually becomes independent through creating, they do not have to submit their mind to the beliefs/practices of others. As an evolved being, their sustenance becomes a product of their imagination; in a certain sense, their internal world and their external world combine.

"It is the coming together of yin and yang that allows creation. The ability to create is a human's greatest gift."

—John Chang[4]

From an alchemical point of view, individuals at this level of awareness are consistently creating because they have sustained an awareness above fusion. It is theorized that energetically, during the creative process, the subtle yin (feminine) and yang (masculine) energies merge together in the cranium. Therefore, it is possible that the reason individuals who have opened the seventh sacred disc are always creating is because they have a sustained awareness beyond the sixth chakra. When sustaining awareness beyond the sixth sacred disc, the individual is maintaining a conscious state of merged yin and yang.

While the practice of creation can be seen as the ultimate expression of man, I would not necessarily place it above an athlete or someone that has found soul-purpose.

Measuring Intelligence

Because there are so many paths when it comes to developing one's concentration and activating the spirit, some people can be quite advanced without even knowing what chakras are. In this situation, I will usually ask the individual to close their eyes. If they only see darkness, then I would assume that they are not very advanced. However, if they see various geometric shapes and patterns, then I believe they are quite advanced, because this is the light of the soul. As mentioned, with relation to the three dan tiens, the Daoists will measure one's intelligence by first looking at the quality of their teeth, then their skin, and then finally their eyes. One's level of intelligence/self-mastery is also characterized by the breath. When an individual has mastery over their mind, their body is able to reach deeper states of relaxation—it is like their body is asleep while they are awake. During these states, the breath is slow and deep, and can even sound like snoring. Scientifically these states can be measured by brainwave activity labeled in categories known as alpha, beta, theta, delta, and gamma.

Fountain of Youth

Appearing in literature, since before the 5th century BCE[5], the legendary Fountain of Youth is said to be a mythical spring that restores the youth of anyone who bathes in its waters. Many dream of finding the sacred Fountain of Youth and retaining their youthfulness into old age. However, because of the lack of information surrounding the fountain, many come to believe that the Fountain of Youth is just a fable and not actually reachable.

The truth is that the Fountain of Youth is real and does exist. However, it is not a secret fountain to be found in some far-off place, but instead actually exists within each of us. If one looks around, they may notice that many people look older with age, however, they may also notice that a very few select individuals retain their youthfulness and actually become more refined with age. This is because they have attained Fountain of Youth. The Fountain of Youth is an *internal attainment* related to self-refinement/cultivation. One reaches the Fountain of Youth not through external exploration but through developing their awareness, the spirit. Therefore, the Fountain of Youth is a conscious evolutionary attainment.

The Fountain of Youth allows the body to raise and *recycle* the vital energy of the body that is normally led downward because of gravity and expended through reproduction and exertion. Gravity is what causes individuals to age and die, but a person can hinder its effects and increase their lifespan by following the heart and consistently refining their concentration. When all seven major disks are open, then the central channel, sushumna, is clear. Sushumna allows the body's liquid vital energy to flow up from the lower dan tien and through the sacred disks to the top of the head, where there is an opening that allows the vital energy to flow back down over the face and down the body. The body becomes like a fountain. This is recycling the vital energy and restoring the body's youthfulness. Completing this process allows a person to retain their essence and live youthfully for a long time. Normally, the life force energy is not raised and is exhausted through day-to-day activities and continuous sexual intercourse.

The entire body is the fountain, and the top of the head is the spout. Because of this active recycling process, individuals look fresh and renewed. Many yogic masters are noted to have appeared almost shiny and wet—this is why. Upon being recycled, the liquid vital energy flowing out of the top of the head creates the sensation of a fountain flowing down the head and onto the face.

The Fountain of Youth is most effective when the individual has their kundalini (energy) raised. Those who regularly partake in activities that cause them to "power up" or, in other words, reside in a concentration-based state, are utilizing the Fountain of Youth to a higher potential. A few great masters in China like Chang San Geng and Bhodhidharma have even been attributed to have lived 200 years.[6]

Similar to the halo, many of the people who attain this achievement are not actually sensitive to it. The vital energy flowing down the body is very subtle. However, those who attain this achievement through meditation will be sensitive to the energy which is flowing down the face and body from the top of the head. This is a sensation related to activating the seventh major chakra. For them, it feels like a liquid bath on the face and especially on facial hair because the liquid energy comes together there, just like water does when washing one's face.

Practitioners in China do a certain exercise for longevity and spiritual growth which has its roots originating from an understanding of the Fountain of Youth. The exercise is a little bit strange, but is primarily noted for longevity and enhancing spiritual growth. In order to do the exercise, one breathes in and tightens the scrotum/anus area, then breathes out and releases. This is done repetitively for about 1-2 minutes.

The Holy Grail

"Drink this, all of you; for this is My blood of the covenant, which is poured out for many for the forgiveness of sins. I tell you, I shall not drink again of the fruit of the vine until I drink it new with you in My Father's kingdom."

–Matthew (26:27-29)

The legendary "Holy Grail" is a recurring theme throughout history, having deep connections with spirituality and religion. The Holy Grail is most often associated with early medieval literary traditions, and also with the "Holy Chalice" that was believed to be used by Jesus Christ himself to serve wine at the Last Supper. It is also believed that drinking from the Holy Grail endows individuals with supernatural powers.

Many often wonder, where is the Holy Grail located? In truth, however, the legendary Holy Grail is not something to be found hidden away in some secret vault under the Vatican. The legendary Holy Grail is actually not a physical object at all, but an occurrence and an experience to be attained. Similar to the Fountain of Youth, the Holy Grail is actually a metaphor describing an internal phenomenon; it is a conscious evolutionary attainment within the reach of all individuals.

Looking at the ancient yogic texts in India and China, one can often find descriptions of a powerful occurrence at the moment of Samadhi, also known as the breathless state: the tongue automatically folds backwards into the back of the mouth making contact with the uvula (dangling tissue in the back of the throat).

According to texts when the practitioner enters into the state of Samadhi, the tongue automatically folds back and makes direct contact with the uvula, creating a connection both physically and energetically. At this stage, the tongue begins to receive drips of a special liquid secreted from the brain. This elixir of life, commonly referred to as the "sweet nectar" or as "amrit," brings the practitioner powerful sensations of ecstasy and fullness. Drop by drop, this is the experience of drinking from the Holy Grail. In India, the yogis refer to this experience as Khechari Mudra.

Because true Khechari Mudra is a highly regarded technique among yogic circles, some have actually developed specific methods to replicate the natural process. These techniques consist of continually cutting small slits in the flesh underneath the tongue (the frenulum), allowing the tongue to stretch back further and further, and eventually make direct contact with the uvula. While interesting, these techniques are not recommended and can often even be dangerous to the practitioner, leading to possible infection. As a human being consciously evolves, this tissue that connects the tongue to the bottom of the mouth will decline away naturally. Understanding this process, one realizes that the freedom of the tongue is actually an evolutionary attribute, as strange as it sounds. When true Samadhi is attained, the master will be ready.

Besides being a glorified experience, drinking from the Holy Grail also serves a very functional purpose for the practitioner. Eventually, when a master achieves true self-mastery and attains the breathless state, they become able to reside in complete concentration continually for very long periods of time: days, weeks, or sometimes even months. During these long periods of time, the body enters into a state of suspended animation. The reason that the body can sustain itself without food is because of the Holy Grail/Khechari Mudra phenomenon. The drips of liquid that are continually absorbed by the tongue from the uvula actually provide nutrients to the practitioner and sustain their physical form.

Suspended Animation

In the West, conventional understanding declares that the human body can sustain itself for 8 weeks without food, 3-5 days without water, and 3-4 minutes without air. However, many traditions around the world would disagree, and instead claim that man has the innate ability to enter into a state of "suspended animation" for long periods of time. It is alchemically understood that suspended animation can be consciously induced when an individual is able to sustain concentration beyond thought processes. Through self-mastery, by slowing down the mind, one induces a dramatic decline in the breath and bodily functions. By doing so, they consciously put their body into a state of suspended animation—this is commonly referred to as "voluntary trance" or Samadhi.

"In the initial states of God-contact (*sabikalpa samadhi*) the devotee's consciousness merges with the Cosmic Spirit; his life force is withdrawn from the body, which appears "dead," or motionless and rigid. The yogi is fully aware of his bodily condition of suspended animation. As he progresses to higher spiritual states (*nirbikalpa samadhi*), however, he communes with God without bodily fixation, and in his ordinary waking consciousness, even in the midst of exacting worldly duties."

-Paramhansa Yogananda[7]

When looking at India, it is historically a common practice for yogis to actually be buried alive for days at a time. However, in the last 30 years there have been so many fatalities among inadequately trained holy men attempting this feat that the Indian authorities have stopped it completely.[8] Scientifically, because of the lack of air available, a normal human is only expected to live for ten minutes to an hour if buried alive.

"Colonel Townshend could seemingly 'die' whenever he pleased. Using the power of his mind he would stop his heart from beating; there were no signs of breathing, and his whole body would become as cold and stiff as death itself. His features were shrunk and colorless, and his eyes distant and cold. He would remain in this state for many hours and then slowly revive. According to his doctor, Dr. Cheyne, Colonel Townsend's own description of the phenomenon was that he could 'die or expire when he pleased; and yet by an effort of both mind and body, or somehow, he could come to life again'. On one occasion three medical men witnessed his phenomena, one of whom kept his hand on the Colonel's heart, another held his wrist, and the third put a mirror in front of his lips. They found that all traces of breathing and pulse gradually stopped. So convinced were they that he was in fact dead, that they were ready to leave the room when they noticed some signs of life appearing, and slowly he revived."[9]

When researching suspended animation, a common theme is that the body actually becomes ghostly and dead looking. The description of Colonel Townshend is very similar to Alexandra David-Neel's description of the monks in Tibet. Alexandra David-Neel wrote about how the community members would go to the head monk to ask specific questions. In order to retrieve information, the master would close his eyes and his body would become white and stiff, like a dead body, very similar to the description of Colonel Townshend.[10] One discrepancy, however, is that Alexandra David-Neel points out that when the monks are in this hollow state of suspended animation they cannot be touched. She points out that the shock from being touched will cause them to die. In *Initiation into Hermetics*, Franz Bardon also describes that one cannot be touched while in this state. He explains that the shock induced from touching the body can destroy the cord that connects the subtle body to the physical body, resulting in death.[11] Personally, I believe that the physical form becomes white and life-less appearing because the etheric body has separated from it. The etheric body contains the life force that sustains the physical form, and so when it is detached, the body loses both life and color.

"In time, something very strange happened. I could spend longer and longer periods in meditation, once I did not move for eight days. And my consciousness would fly all over the world as I desired."

–John Chang[12]

Suspended animation is not something that I have been able to attain personally, however, because of wide-spread accounts I do believe it to be possible. Notable personal accounts of suspended animation include John Chang, Franz Bardon, Wang Liping, Alexandra David-Neel's Tibetan monks, Jiang Feng, and Chunyi Lin. More publically notable candidates include Prahlad Jani and "Buddha Boy."

Lu Dogbin 100 Character Tablet

Lu Dogbin, born around 798 CE, was the central figure of an ancient Chinese group known as the "Eight Immortals." The Eight Immortals are one of the most legendary groups not only in the history of the Daoist religion but in all of Chinese history. For the purpose of transmitting his wisdom, master Lu Dogbin created the *100 Character Tablet*. This profound tablet carries alchemical secrets about human development. Once decoded, it serves as a map, illustrating the path of ascension towards heavenly awareness.

养 气 忘 言 守

Nurturing energy, forget words and guard it.

降 心 为 不 为

Conquer the mind, act effortlessly.

动 静 知 宗 祖

In movement and stillness, know your true self.

无 事 更 寻 谁

There is nothing to search for; whom else do you seek?

真 常 须 应 物

The external self must respond to the world

应 物 要 不 迷

When responding, don't get attached and lost.

不 迷 性 自 住

When you don't get confused, your nature is naturally stable,

性 住 气 自 回

When your nature is stable, energy naturally returns.

气 回 丹 自 结

When energy returns, elixir spontaneously crystallizes,

壶 中 配 坎 离

In the pot pairing water and fire.

阴 阳 生 反 复

Yin and yang arise, alternating over and over again,

普 化 一 声 雷

Everywhere producing the sound of thunder.

白 云 朝 顶 上

White clouds assemble on the summit,

甘 露 洒 须 弥

Sweet dew sprinkles the holy mountain.

自 饮 长 生酒

Having drunk the wine of longevity,

逍 遥 谁 得知

You wander free; who can know you?

坐 听 无 弦 曲

You sit and listen to string-less melody,

明 通 造化机

You clearly understand the mechanism of creation.

都 来 二 十句

The whole of these twenty verses,

端 的 上 天

Is a ladder straight to heaven.

Analysing the Tablet

When analyzing the tablet, one can find connections with different occurrences that arise throughout the process of conscious evolution. Much of the tablet can be understood openly, and any direct knowing/understanding gained from reading Lu Dogbin's words should be treasured. The following analysis is only meant to help.

Nurturing energy, forget words and guard it.

Conquer the mind, act effortlessly.

(Lines 1–2)

When looking at the last words of the first line, "guard it," there is a direct connection with master Laozi's phrase, "Guard the One." In the Daoist theory of self-cultivation "Guarding the One" is defined as non-action, and means keeping the body empty and pure from defilements.[1] This often consists of abandoning desires, or "conquering the mind."

When observing the second line, the "mind" is referring to both one's thoughts and emotions. The Chinese characters for this line are 降 心 为 不 为. The characters place an emphasis on taming the emotions by doing non-doing (relaxation observation). Whereby 降 refers to lowering or at ease. 心 refers to one's mind that is full of thoughts and emotion. These first two characters show that one should take precedence towards easing their thoughts and emotions. With this, one may, 为 不 为, "act effortlessly."

In movement and stillness, know your true self,

There is nothing to search for; whom else do you seek?

(Lines 3–4)

As mentioned previously, knowing the true self cultivates an expanded experiential awareness: a silence. It is the true self, the immortal self, a source of life that persists beyond the cycle of continuous death and rebirth.

> *The external self must respond to the world,*
> *When responding, don't get attached and lost.*
>
> (Lines 5-6)

One must respond, a.k.a. take "responsibility," to the world in order to remain in balance while on Earth. "The truest measure is to deal with things," as Lao Tzu says. Those that deal with things erase entanglement, and lay the necessary foundation in order to consciously rise from the earthly plane towards the heavenly. This is the foundation of silence that is created through harmony.

When looking at the second line, it is important when responding not to get attached to the point of losing touch with the eternal self; the notion is to create harmony without becoming lost.

> *When you don't get confused, your nature is naturally stable,*
> *When your nature is stable, energy naturally returns.*
>
> (Lines 7-8)

Having a stable nature is directly referring to one's control in regards to their thoughts and emotions. A deeper understanding of the second line can be gained when one simplifies the Chinese characters.

Chinese: 性 住 气 自 回

Whereby 性 refers to "emotion" or "emotion pattern; 住 refers to "settled", 气 refers to "the energy", 自 refers to "by itself" and 回 refers to "return".

The early Daoist writings attributed to Tianyinzi view the oppositions of joy and anger, sadness and happiness, love, hate, and desire, as the seven perversions of the emotions. It is taught that ridding oneself of the seven perversions creates a foundation so that one may establish immortality (spirit immortal).[2] They are seen as states of disharmony, like a corruption or a distortion in a person that needs to be tamed, and that can over time drain one's energy, leading to a shorter lifespan. By maintaining a stable nature, the energy will begin to return by itself.

> *When energy returns, elixir spontaneously crystallizes,*
> *In the pot pairing water and fire.*
> (Lines 9–10)

The first line describes the lower dan tien becoming cultivated naturally. The Chinese characters for line 9, 气 回 丹 自 结, explain that the "elixir field" is reconstituted when energy returns. Whereby 丹 refers to Dan Tian, which is loosely translated as elixir field or energy center, 自 refers to self, and 结 refers to being settled. The energy returning is accumulating in and cultivating the lower dan tien. As discussed in a previous section, because of its importance as a "foundation," the cultivation of the lower dan tien is also the primary aim of many Daoist breathing techniques.

> *"Yin and yang arise, alternating over and over again,*
> *Everywhere producing the sound of thunder."*
> (Lines 11–12)

Line 11 refers to the yin and yang energies combining at the sixth chakra point. At this point, the kundalini energies finally form the "yoga," or union, coming together and alternating. In Indian diagrams, this process is visually depicted by the two serpent heads coming together on the forehead.

Line 11 Chinese characters: 阴阳生反复:

This line means, "Yin-Yang is continually reborn." Whereby Yin-Yang (阴阳) refers to the Taiji diagram that shows continued movement of Yin and Yang as they are renewed and transformed, 生 refers to "born", and 反复 refers to "continually". Yin and yang are connected in the Tai Chi diagram, flowing into one another—Yang becoming yin, and yin becoming yang.

Line 12, that describes thunder being produced everywhere, is the result of the fusion of the yin and yang energies. This is the birth of "electric qi," also known in the Daoist traditions as *Houtian Fusion*. The Chinese characters for line 12 are: 普化一声雷.

Line 12 can be more accurately translated to mean,

"The mundane is transformed in one clap of thunder."

Whereby 普 refers to common or mundane, and 化 refers to transform. Personally, I find that line 12 is the most significant line on the tablet. This is the birth of spirit and a transformation beyond a normal or mundane existence. With the sixth chakra awakened, the sexual energy is now able to reside in the brain and stimulate spirit: this marks the beginning of the "Shen" spiritual consciousness.

"White clouds assemble at the summit."

(Line 13)

The white clouds assembling at the summit are referring to the light of shen that is becoming apparent in the third dan tien. If you look closely at the Neijing Tu diagram, the river (sexual energy) flows and accumulates at the top of the head; this is, "the white clouds assembling at the summit." Shen is the light that shifts the conscious experience, brightening a person's reality from the inside out.

"Sweet dew baths the polar mountain."

(Line 14)

After opening the sixth chakra, one begins activating the seventh "crown" chakra. With all seven chakras activated, the major channel (Sushumna) is clear and the vital energy is able to flow up towards the top of the head. The crown at the top of the head opens and allows the vital energy to flow down the body. The "polar mountain" that is being referred to is an individual's face. The "sweet dew" that is bathing the polar mountain is referring to the vital energy flowing out from the top of the head and down the body, most noticeably down the face: this is because the face is very sensitive. Line 14 is a description of the Fountain of Youth. As the vital energy is a liquid, the Fountain of Youth phenomenon creates the feeling of drops of dew continually sliding down the face. This phenomenon is the vital energy being recycled, or recirculated, and keeping the body young.

"Having drunk the wine of longevity,
You wander free; who cares?
You sit and listen to string-less melody,
You clearly understand the mechanism of creation."

(Lines 15–18)

The "wine of longevity" is the Daoist way of describing the experience of drinking from the Holy Grail[3] that is stimulated by the spirit. The "wine" is the golden nectar, "amrit," that flows directly from the awakened pineal gland.

The "string-less melody" is the ability to perceive life with an open mind. This is similar to how the Tibetan Dzogchen tradition explains a state of mind where a person can look at an object and perceive it as empty. The object is empty in the sense that no thoughts or opinions are placed on it and the object is perceived purely as it is. The description of this state of perception gives insight into the nature of a highly intelligent person. The individual perceives life more clearly without the un-mastered sense of thought obstructing the inflow of experience. This pure perception of the nature of reality allows the individual to have a clear and accurate understanding of the world. This clarity also leads those at this stage of development to begin partaking in the process of creation; their innovations are a result of "seeing."

ALCHEMICAL EVOLUTION
[The Path of the Sage]

During one's conscious progression, the chakras will be developing in the background, and those who meditate regularly will come into contact with them experientially. However, as with the previous chapters, it is not necessary to be in contact with them in order for them to develop. It is more essential to be aware of one's mutable experience and to be taking steps forward (self-realization/alchemy). For those that only train meditation and alchemical practices, it is recommended to practice for 45 minutes twice per day.

"Yoga is a technology. If you learn to use it, it works—no matter where you come from or what you believe in or do not believe in."

–Sadhguru

The true goal of the alchemist is to open the major chakras, leading to an amplification of the nervous system, lighting the mind on fire and unlocking the spirit. Through realization one becomes able to be what one wants to be, to become able to work at any chosen thing all day and night without stopping.

Masters in the past have designed specific methods and techniques aimed solely towards activating the etheric body and awakening one's dormant potential, allowing the individual to reach higher states of concentration. Many techniques are focused directly towards developing specific regions of the etheric body. In the video game of an alchemist's existence, the etheric body is the game itself, and the chakras are the levels.

Inspire = To Animate

The main purpose of alchemical training is to first open the first six major chakras (shat-chakras) along the spine. Climbing the spine through developing the chakras intensifies one's concentration.

Techniques are Not the Only Way

Considering conscious ascension is the most important endeavor a human being can undergo, many societies and lineages around the world have tried to encrypt their practices, hiding them away in secrecy. This high level of exaltation placed upon spiritual practices cause individuals to lose a fundamental understanding of spirituality and one's evolution towards enlightenment. They begin to believe that the alchemical practices are the 'only' way towards spiritual growth and the heavenly experience. This limited understanding towards spirituality takes expansion out of their hands, and causes them to believe they need a secret key. In the process of conscious evolution, there are no secret locks or keys—there are tools.

In the process of self-discovery, first came natural evolution, then meditation, and then finally alchemical techniques. Through observing and understanding spiritual states of consciousness obtained through natural evolution, the practice of meditation was developed. Furthermore, alchemical techniques were derived from learning about the subtle aspects of life with an awareness gained through the consistent practice of meditation. Furthermore, advanced techniques and methods were created by advanced meditators as a result of their expanded understanding and interactions with the etheric body.

It is advantageous to consider soul-purpose and meditation as support beams that one should utilize while they are practicing techniques. The simplicity of refining concentration through meditation and soul-purpose are operating processes that are beyond comprehension. Techniques are effective, but they are the most derived source of training. For this reason, it is possible that a person can train complicated techniques for a long period of time and not make true progress because they are not connecting the correct dots that would naturally be connected. Therefore, anyone who practices alchemical techniques should supplement them with at least some regular meditation practice or soul-purpose to be sure they are progressing properly. This is to ensure consistent, and well-rounded progress. For example, if one is consistently using the AUM mantra to awaken higher chakras, but at the same time they still have dormant lower chakras, then, even if they did awaken a higher chakra, the kundalini would not be able to reach the higher awakened chakra. As a result, there is very little stopping the awakened center from just becoming dormant again, wasting the individual's efforts. In all natural efforts involving concentration, the kundalini will always rise from the bottom up.

Lastly, during training it is important to avoid judging oneself while becoming acquainted with the etheric body. One should remain detached to the various sensations that arise, and instead maintain focus on the practice itself. The sensations arise from the practice, so becoming attached to the sensations can deviate one from the practice itself. Teachers will often say, "The less one expects, the better."

Awakening is found in Duality

Alchemical techniques and methods were created for a specific purpose and they are not all encompassing; techniques and methods have limitations. They are tools, but they are tools that were designed for a specific purpose. For this reason, it is important to stay in balance with nature by avoiding losing balance in one's outward life. Often times individuals quit their lifestyle in order to go to the mountains for long term training, but during their training they can't stop thinking about what they are going to do in the future, or if they are making progress currently, or if this sensation means this or that. Ultimately, I believe that their practices do not yield much benefit because they are in a state of fright. A person needs to have already made great achievement (breathless state) in order to be ready for this type of training (cave meditation). A path of balance is similar to the Buddhist "Middle Way."

Meditation

Too young to meditate...
Too bad to meditate....
Too in love to meditate...
Too busy to meditate...
Too worried to meditate...
Too sick to meditate...
Too excited to meditate...
Too tired to meditate...
Too late to meditate...
-Buddha

Why Meditation?

Student: Why do we meditate?
Master: Meditation is everything.

Meditation is similar to the natural path, awareness over mind and thinking—awareness is used to break through and become able to "see."

Through concentration, individuals refine their awareness and realize spiritual evolution. Self-refinement can occur when one is involved with playing sports, martial arts, creating music, writing, etc. This can be any activity that enlivens a person's spirit-soul (a.k.a.

soul-purpose). However, it was discovered that it is also possible for one to refine their awareness and undergo self-refinement without having to do any particular activity outwardly. One can become in touch with the very processes behind concentration and spiritual evolution.

Meditation is self-refinement through non-doing. The pitfall to meditation is when one lacks responsibility/destiny—the outward pursuit of silence.

Meditation is like an anchor, connecting one with their soul-awareness so that they do not drift too far away. Meditation works to purify the soul by developing the etheric body activating the spirit and attaining higher conscious states. A regular practice upgrades intelligence, and launches an individual into a more concentrated level of being. The beauty of meditation is that with proper practice it does not matter where one is in life, they will make conscious evolutionary progress. It is the instant and direct access to the giver of life that makes meditation a most powerful tool for helping to lead individuals towards truth in their outward lives. A consistent daily practice of meditation is like holding one's hand and walking them straight to the gates of heaven.

Alone = All One

By bringing one into a more direct experience with reality, the thoughts of the past and the future have less leverage over the individual's awareness and one becomes able to experience the present moment with more intensity. Transforming from the inside also causes one to also transform on the outside. A clear state of mind brings consistent realization about oneself in relation to their present situation, bringing more self-control, understanding, and the ability to consciously direct oneself in life.

"The ultimate goal is to become one with God, to become a god. We are gods, but we are not aware of it. We suffer from a self-inflicted amnesia. The aim is to reawaken that which we have always been and we shall always be."

–Daskalos

Yogis would say, "The soul is the god." Meditation practice can be considered a direct way to worship spiritual awareness. Daily practice serves as both a guide and a symbol of devotion towards one's conscious evolution. With regular practice, the practitioner naturally seeks the meditative-state externally as well as internally. This experience is associated with the Daoist idea of emptiness.

How to Meditate

The body, mind, and spirit are connected; they are often seen as the trinity of one's being. In meditation practice, one is relaxing the body and releasing stray thoughts in order to set precedence to and refine the spirit awareness. By letting the body to become still and allowing the thoughts to flow by, one awakens and purifies their spirit. From this natural state of concentration, various sensations and experiences associated with purification begin to arise.

Meditation - The Breath

The practice of meditation begins with sitting down, relaxing the body, and taking a few deep breaths. Taking a few slow, deep breaths is an important preliminary so that the mind and body are able to become relaxed. The breath has a direct connection with the mind, so a slow, deep, and encompassing breath is the sign of a restful and controlled mind. The lower section of the lungs represents the physical, the middle is emotional, and the upper is mental. So a few slow, deep breaths help relax the physical body and prepare for meditation. Many people regularly take short and small breaths during the day that are isolated in the upper chest because of mental tension.

During meditation practice the breath will slow down naturally. This is because the breath is connected to the mind, so slowing down the mind activity will also slow down the breath. Certain Zen meditation practices purposefully focus on slowing down the breath in order to slow down the mind and achieve deep meditation states. However, these methods of meditation are contrived in a way, and it is better to master the awareness directly. If one simply rests in awareness, the breath will slow down automatically as deeper states of concentration are achieved.

Many serious meditators seek to reach the breathless state. By completely transcending the mind, the breath itself also comes to a complete halt. This is connected to the divine experience of being "reborn."

> Jesus replied, "Very truly I tell you, no one can see the kingdom of God unless they are born again."
> "How can someone be born when they are old?" Nicodemus asked. "Surely they cannot enter a second time into their mother's womb to be born!"
> Jesus answered, "Very truly I tell you, no one can enter the kingdom of God unless they are born of Water and the Spirit. Flesh gives birth to flesh, but the Spirit gives birth to spirit."
> (John 3:3-6)

It is referred to as birth into the "Kingdom of God." The idea is that by transcending any beliefs or thoughts of who one is, the practitioner literally becomes who they are experientially. It is an experiential state of self-mastery equated with heaven.

Master and Disciple

Student:
Master, what are the senses?

Master:
Hm... Man is endowed with six senses.
To feel, smell, taste, hear, see, and last but not least, most people are unaware of it, "to think."

Life begins when a Soul enters a physical body to give it life. It is alive because he/she can "feel."

Feeling is the first sense.

Man is made of material nature—commonly known as Earth being. Therefore, our physical body belongs to the Earth element which gives us the sense of odor. Odor is a sense of smell, and is the 2nd sense.

Without the sense of smell, u cannot taste. When you drink bitter medicine, you have nipped or pinched your nose in order to eclipse the taste.

And with the birth of the sense of smell, the third sense, taste, is created. Taste is from the element of water or liquid.

From taste, a subtle sense is developed as an auditory sense vibration in the Air. It is a sound wave. A frequency of auditory sense. Thus, our hearing is formed. To hear is the 4th sense.

From hearing, or sound wave, a more refine light is manifested. Sound to sight.

Sight is the Fifth Sense.

A light of the fire element for us to see.

Last but not least, the fire that turned to light to give sight, further evolved into subtler energies known to man as mind—the thoughtform.

A thinking faculty of cognition, perspective, and discrimination.

A thinking man. It lights up your life.

Amongst the senses, the feeling and thinking centers are the most significant.

These are the six senses.

Soul:
The feeling starts from our Soul, which is Absolute.

The Elements:

Smell represents the body's odor (Earth).

Taste is water (liquid).

Sound or hearing is air or gaseos.

Sight is of the fire or igniteous.

Spirit:
The mind, or thoughtforms, also known as our thinking process, is of the Light (spirit) which is infinite.

Only those who are in control of their senses is a Master.

And with this mastery, the possibilities for self-realization and enlightenment become attainable.

Of the seven chakras, the two primary chakras are the first chakra and the seventh chakra. When considering the six senses, the first chakra represents the body/feeling and the seventh chakra represents thought. Because the first center is so important, it is very helpful for one to remain still and move as little as possible during meditation. Sitting still can be very painful over long periods of time; many people will not even be able to sit for one hour at a time. However, with practice it becomes more natural.

For those that have difficulty remaining still because of discomfort, a technique to try is to simply observe the nature of the pain that is being felt, and to realize its illusory nature. There is a constant wheel of pain to pleasure and pleasure to pain occurring within the body. Watch the wheel circulating inside you with detachment, and attain mastery of the body and of the universe. Meditation is two-fold. It is physical and mental; observe pain and observe thoughts, do not get sucked into thoughts, do not be overthrown by pain. Similarly, the "Ice Man," Wim Hof, would immerse himself in freezing cold lakes in order to invigorate his senses and gain mastery over his body-mind.

Sitting Postures – The Structure of the Temple

Traditionally, meditation training is practiced from a sitting posture. However, an individual should never feel limited because of posture; one should accompany what is comfortable for their body. Many Westerners are commonly advised to begin practicing in a chair.

Whenever possible, it is important to keep the spine straight and erect. This is because the purpose of meditation is to raise the energy from the lower section of the spine upwards during concentration, thus activating the chakras along the spine. If the spine is straight, then there are no kinks and the energy is able to flow unobstructed.

Place hands on the legs or lap, with both hands positioned in a chosen mudra (discussed later). The spine is kept straight like a column of coins and the shoulders are stretched out like the wings of a vulture in order to keep from hunching forward. The chin should be very slightly pressed in towards the larynx, so as to allow energy to flow into the head.[1]

The various sitting postures augment different areas of the etheric body. A very wide variety of postures and their effects on the etheric body have been studied and recorded in detail by the Indian yogis. In Kriya yoga, for example, they have diagrams showing where each different posture concentrates energy on the etheric body. When considering meditation, the three most dominant sitting postures are: normal sitting, half-lotus, and full-lotus. Each of these postures shift concentrations of awareness to different locations of the etheric body. By raising the energy to higher locations, the awareness intensifies, increasing the effectiveness of meditation practice.

Augmentation Locations:

Full-Lotus—Heaven—Top of Head
Half-Lotus—Humanity—Chest
Cross-Legged Sitting—Earth—Stomach

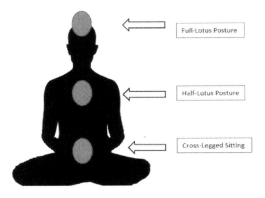

Full-lotus posture is when the practitioner sits with both legs folded in a position so that the top of each foot is resting upside-down on top of each opposite thigh. The sole of each foot should be facing upwards. The hands are usually then placed palms down on the knees. Engaging in a proper full-lotus position will naturally straighten and align the curvature of the back, making it the ideal position for long term meditation. The full-lotus posture is the most powerful meditation position because it raises the energy to the top of the head, helping to expand one's awareness beyond the mind. Note: while one is training sitting meditation, their subtle body will enter into full-lotus position naturally, whether they are aware of it or not.

Half-lotus is when only one foot rests on top of the opposite thigh, while the other foot rests under the opposite thigh.

If the practitioner cannot sit in half-lotus, they can sit with their legs crossed normally. While the energy may be focused in lower centers, normal cross-legged sitting is actually a very effective posture. A practitioner sitting in this way will still make significant progress, especially if they incorporate a hand mudra (discussed later).

Often times, teachers will tell their students to practice in the regular cross-legged sitting position initially because it naturally opens up the hips. Overtime, this helps practitioners to gradually progress towards the half-lotus and then finally into the full-lotus posture. However, it is important not to strain the knees and to be patient with oneself while they are developing flexibility through continual practice. One should never force a posture, instead they should allow them to come naturally.

Flexibility has a direct connection to conscious awareness. As a result, the more advanced meditation postures will come naturally as the conscious awareness of the individual expands. As the practitioner gains more self-mastery, they develop less and less tension in their body and eventually embody a state of complete ease. This process naturally causes the body to become more flexible over time. When individuals eventually reach the sixth and seventh chakras, they will automatically be able to naturally go into the full-lotus posture during meditation. This is because flexibility is linked to consciousness. The Indian practice of Yoga uses stretching exercises in order to help one ascend in consciousness and promote healing. They use stretching postures in order to relax the body/mind in an effort to reach higher states of consciousness. Meditation does the same thing, but the other way around. Meditation directly works to expand one's consciousness, and as a result, the body becomes more flexible.

Also, because of the body-mind connection, it is important to keep the body perfectly still during meditation in order to keep the mind grounded. It is about releasing all tension and need for movement. When the mind becomes still, the breath stops; when the body is still, the mind becomes still.

MUDRAS – The Hand of Awareness

Those who are not able to meditate in the full-lotus position, can implement a hand mudra. A hand mudra raises the resting awareness of the sitting postures, thus increasing the effectiveness of the meditation. Through the use of a hand mudra during meditation one can derive the benefits of the full-lotus posture without having to be highly flexible. Whenever possible, hand mudras are to be utilized during the practice of meditation or any other alchemical techniques.

The most important aspect of the various hand mudras is the thumb. The thumb represents the spine, and the tip of the thumb coincides with the top of the head. By utilizing a hand mudra that touches the tip of the thumb, one is circulating energy in that location and raising awareness to the top of the head. By doing this, one is deriving the benefits of the full-lotus posture. When the awareness rests on the top of the head, the meditator is better able to be aware of the mind and when it drifts, it increases the practitioner's time in awareness and the effectiveness of the meditation practice.

There are three primary variations of hand mudras, which one can employ based on comfort. The first two are very common and are used by practitioners around the world, and the last one is less common.

The first hand mudra connects the tip of the thumb with the tip of the pointer finger, resting the hands with the palms facing upward.

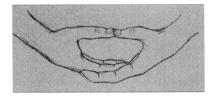

The second mudra, often used in Zen meditation, is performed by placing the right hand over the left hand with both palms facing upwards and connecting the tips of the thumbs.

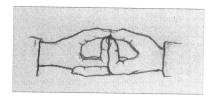

The last hand mudra is a combination of the previous two, and is known as Dhyana Mudra. It is a sacred mudra performed by placing the right hand over the left hand and connecting the two thumbs, but then also raising the two pointer fingers so that they connect with the tips of the thumbs.

Meditation - The Awareness

Throughout all of the paths of ascension, whether it be alchemical, soul-purpose, or meditation, it is the awareness that is being trained.

Awareness is both the path and the destination.
–Zen Proverb.

Below, is a section from The Secret of the Golden Flower. The Secret of the Golden Flower is very ancient. It is one of the most ancient treatises in the world, possibly dating back more than 25 centuries old.

The Secret of the Golden Flower
Chapter 2 Part 9

The method used by the ancients for escaping from the world consisted in refining away the dregs of yin in order to return to the pure Qian. It is just a matter of dissolving the lower self (earthly po-soul) and completing the higher self (celestial hun-soul). Turning the light around is the method of dissolving yin and controlling the lower self. Except for the secret of turning the light around, there is no other exercise to return to Qian. The light itself is Qian; to turn it around is to return to it. Just persist in this method, and naturally vitality-water will be sufficient, spirit-fire will ignite, intent-earth will stabilize and thus the holy embryo gestates.[2]

Returning to Qian is returning to awareness. The light itself is Qian, and light is the ability to see. When one is realizing themselves through soul-purpose, as Tian De explained, they are returning to Qian.

The awareness is the spiritual potential of an individual; its development increases concentration, clarity, and potential. The accuracy and efficiency behind every action or effort made by a person is subject to the development of their awareness. By working with and intensifying that which is perceiving the reality, meditation practice is increasing the proficiency of everything that one does.

Bodhidharma

Bodhidharma's disciple Eka asked, "If someone is committed to seeking the Buddha's Way, what methods for training should he give heed to?"

Bodhidharma replied, "Since meditation

embraces all methods and practices, I call it the essential one."

Eka asked, "How can one single method embrace all practices?"

Bodhidharma replied, "It is the root and source of all methods, all methods are simply products of the mind so, if you are able to thoroughly comprehend what 'real mind' is, then your myriad practices will be fully equipped.

Your 'real mind' is a great tree; its branches, blossoms and fruit all depend completely on the root, even a severed tree will survive if its root is intact whereas a fully grown tree, once detached from its root will die. If you train in the Way with a thorough comprehension of what 'real mind' is, then you will conserve your strength as you easily succeed in realizing Buddhahood but, if you train without thoroughly comprehending what 'real mind' is, then you will squander your efforts to no avail."[3]

In the teachings above, the "real-mind" being referred to, is one's conscious awareness. The reason that meditation embraces all practices and methods is because the practitioner is intensifying their conscious awareness directly. The awareness itself is the potential behind any method or technique that one utilizes. So by directly expanding the awareness itself, one is embracing all methods and practices.

Six sense meditation (commonly taught by the Tibetans) involves concentrating on either taste, feeling, smell, sound, sight, and last but not least, thought.

Many different techniques have been developed centered around this practice. One need only find what is suitable for them. While sitting, one could fixate their awareness on a particular sound that they hear in the background and concentrate on it continuously. A common meditation involving sound is to simply observe the breath going in and out (see side note). The "Ice Man," Wim Hof, immersed himself in the cold in order to concentrate awareness on the sense of feeling. If exercising awareness through the visual sense, one could concentrate on a particular object placed in front of them, continuously observing that object. A common technique is staring at a candle and then closing the eyes and staring at the after-image created.

Side Note: In India there are 112 different ancient meditation techniques attributed to Lord Shiva. One of these techniques refer to focusing on the gap between the in-breath and the out-breath.[4] The idea behind this meditation is that, this momentary pause is important because a profound awareness is born there. The reason for this is because of prana (energy) circulation. The prana rises up the body with the in-breath and then back down the body with the out-breath. The importance of the short pause between the in-breath and the out-breath is because during this pause the prana will be at the very top of the head. This point at the top of the head is associated with silence, or sustained awareness beyond the mind.

When I first started training, I began with concentrating on sound. I would sit in meditation posture at night and continually sustain awareness on the sound of crickets. After that I moved onto visually staring at objects, and then gradually began meditation centered around mastering the sixth sense: thought. The Tibetans regarded meditation involving the mastery of thought to be the highest form.

"Just sitting cross legged kuan–hsin,

he saw what mind would spin. The

mind immaculate stands firm. The

mind's stained shadows churn." [5]

(Stanza on Bhodidharma)

This quote by Bhodidharma gives insight into the true nature of meditation and of being stable in awareness. Bhodidharma is resting in awareness (mind immaculate) and letting the thoughts (mind stained) pass by without becoming swept away. By allowing the fog to clear away, the practice of meditation brings one closer into true nature

During meditation, while sitting in awareness, one may notice that their thoughts begin to take them far away from the present moment. Thoughts about different fabricated situations constantly relocate the individual away from the present moment. This is viewed as karma by some, because it is taking away from an individual what is most precious, the present moment. This doesn't only happen while sitting in meditation either. During daily life, most of the time individuals are not actually aware of drifting away in thoughts and leaving the present moment, they just sort of come back and then go away again. For this reason, the day-to-day state of mind can be compared to a form of sleep. It takes meditation to realize this.

During meditation, it is normal for one to suddenly come back to awareness and then remember that they are practicing meditation. This occurrence in meditation is referred to as a "blackout," because the individual is literally blacking out in thought, and temporarily losing self-awareness of where they are and what they are doing. The obvious goal of meditation practice is to reach a point where one remains stable in awareness for the entire duration of the practice and does not "blackout." Over time, each individual begins to experience their outer life with a different level of awareness.

While practicing meditation, one simply returns to awareness whenever they lose awareness and "blackout" in thought. The blackouts are not to be viewed as a bad thing, just let them pass and then return to awareness when able. The mind is not separate from oneself, it is an aspect of oneself just like an arm or a leg. Many, however, are constantly straining their minds and do not know how to rest in awareness. It is like a person constantly tensing their arm all day. In meditation one is allowing their mind to relax and setting precedence towards the awareness. The mind is a part of oneself, so it is not possible to use force to achieve stillness or to get frustrated by it. One just lets the thoughts flow through them un-attached while abiding in awareness. The focus is not in doing anything with the body or mind, but instead towards sustaining the awareness. Slowly, with continual practice, the individual becomes more and more in control of themselves and becomes able to stay present in unshaken awareness for long periods of time.

"To clear away random thoughts," he began in reply, "first use formal judgment to deal with them. As soon as a random thought arises, immediately pass judgment on it: either declare it right, or declare it wrong, or declare that this is as far as it goes. Having made this determination, stop right away and do not allow rumination to go on and on. Then random thoughts will vanish by themselves, and in this way you can enter into stillness."[6]

-Wang Liping's Meditation Instructions

It is important to never try to force the mind into quiescence, never try to stop thinking or to deliberately blank out your thoughts. Instead, be as Bhodidharma. Seeing what the mind will spin, let the thoughts just flow like a river while remaining stable in awareness. At first the river is great and powerful, and will drag the practitioner around getting lost in "blackouts", but eventually, and over continual practice, the river narrows and becomes a calm stream just flowing by. Do not restrain the flow of the mind; listen to and acknowledge each thought, but keep going. Another way to look at it is that thoughts are like billboards passing by on the side of a highway, and the meditator is the car.

While practicing, when one returns to awareness after having drifted away in thought, often times it can be beneficial to say a simple mantra like "I Am" to signify to the self that they have returned to conscious awareness.

"The mind for me is like the moon. It doesn't have any light of its own. It has the reflected light from the sun. Like the mind has the reflected Light that comes from the Heart."

–Mooji

The heart can be seen as the center of one's awareness, and when one is able to rest in awareness and not give energy to their thoughts, then they will gradually slow down and allow one to eventually reach silence. In meditation, one watches thoughts as they arise and recede. They are filled with life.

"We are born as an empty cup. Life fills this cup up with wants, needs, and desires. Meditation empties the cup. And then it is filled with something else."

–Thomas

Meditation after Mastery

There comes a point (sixth chakra/See the Light/Spirit Activation) when the practice of meditation becomes able to penetrate thought and the practitioner is able to continuously sustain concentration. After this experience, the meditation practice changes—it becomes similar to watching television, in a way. Alchemical techniques become meaningless and absolute concentration takes primary importance. In Buddhism, this is known as attaining the first level of Samadhi.

Alchemical Methods

Meditation is the primary method for alchemical evolution. Other methods and techniques are designed for a boost; they are not necessarily a central focus.

Mantra – Vibration of Purification

Mantra is the spoken word. With regards to energy work, mantras have been used for a multitude of purposes ranging from worshipping deities, activating yantras[1], or even for casting spells. However, when it comes to conscious expansion, the two main functions of mantras are either to clear the mind or to focus vibrations at target areas of the etheric body.

Mantras aimed towards centering oneself and clearing the mind are utilized during meditation training. While training, the practitioner recites a short phrase, such as "I Am," after regaining consciousness from a "black out" state. The mantra is recited right after one becomes self-aware again, signifying that they are in a state of awareness and continuing their practice. Historically, a useful mantra for this purpose is the "I Am." Considering the practitioner is their awareness, by simply repeating this mantra after a "black out" they signify a return to their awareness. With continual meditation, the mantra is repeated less and less frequently because the practitioner is able to rest in awareness for longer periods of time. Some practitioners actually invent mantras that have no direct meaning, and as a result of their recitation during meditation nothing in particular comes to mind.

The second type of mantra is directed towards purifying specific areas of the etheric body, most notably the sacred disks (chakras). These mantras are the main focus of kundalini tantra alchemical practices, and are repeated constantly for long periods of time, as opposed to the first form of mantra that is only repeated occasionally. While repeating the second type of mantra, the practitioner sounds out the vibrations of the word with each repetition. (for example: OMMMM). When these mantras are sounded out, they create vibrations at target regions of the body that correspond to the major energy centers. The mantras do not need to be shouted, but should be sounded out at a comfortable volume. Through their repetition, the practitioner is utilizing vibrations to shake and gradually awaken the corresponding energy center.

The most powerful mantras are the ones that awaken the chakras in correspondence with the kundalini. For someone that is new to cultivation, they would start by repeating mantras corresponding to the lower chakras. Looking at the etheric body, the lower dan tien is the power supply behind the kundalini. During concentration, the energy rises from the lower dan tien, so the if one is using mantras the goal is to facilitate that rising of the kundalini energy.

A proper training regimen for those training with mantras would be to start with the lowest chakra and use a corresponding mantra 30 minutes daily for two months. Then move onto the next chakra for two months. If practicing mantras daily, one should also be training in meditation/natural progression for well-rounded progress.

The Bija mantras (root mantras) for each major chakra are as follows:

1. Lam (pronounced "Laum")
2. Vam (Pronounced "Vaum")
3. Ram (Pronounced "Raum")
4. Yam (Pronounced "Yaum")
5. Ham (Pronounced "Haum")
6. OM (or "AUM")

By vibrating these mantras out and relaxing the body, one will feel the vibrations in the area of each major chakra they correspond to.

Historical Mantras

NUM

Besides the root mantras, there is the special mantra NUM, which is given to disciples to practice early in their training. It is aimed at the Heart Chakra, the center of one's being, but this mantra shakes all of the chakras. One should start to feel vibrations on their lips while repeating.

Om Mani Padme Hum

This is the most well-known and revered mantra of Tibet. This mantra is aimed towards simultaneously awakening all 6 of the major chakras throughout the spine. When sounding this mantra out in a slow deep manner one will feel where the vibrations are targeting. This mantra breaks down into 6 parts, with each part representing one of the 6 chakras. Om-6th, Ma-1st, Ne-2nd, Pad (pronounced "Pey")-3rd, Me-4th, Hum (pronounced "hung")-5th. By repeating this mantra continuously for long periods of time (20-30 minutes) on a daily basis, individuals will purify and awaken the 6 major sacred disks (chakras) along the spine, eventually allowing them to become able to enter into absolute concentration.[2]

Om Namah Shivaya

This is the most popular ancient mantra from India. People consider it a mantra both for physical and mental healing, which makes sense because similar to the Tibetan mantra, this mantra focuses on awakening the six major chakras a.k.a. wheels of vitality. Many connote the word Shiva to the legendary Indian God-man warrior, however, Shiva literally means: "that which is not." The goal of this mantra is not to gain the favor of an external deity, but instead is a tool to utilize in order to purify one's own chakras and help them enter into non-being.

Similar to the previous mantra, this mantra breaks into six parts: Om-Na-Ma-Shi-Va-Ya. Each part of the mantra corresponds to a particular major chakra. "Nah" -1st, "Mah"-2nd, "She" -3rd, "Vah"-4th, "Yah"-5th, "Aum"-6th. When vibrating out the sounds for long periods of time, the individual will notice that the vibrations focus in the corresponding location. Examples of how to sound out the mantras: VAHHH. YAHHH, AUMMM, and so on.

Ultimately, those training with mantras are primarily concerned with opening the first six major chakras. When the individual is finally able to raise their kundalini from the base chakra to the sixth chakra, they will no longer need any more mantras or techniques, because they will be able to focus one-pointedly beyond the mind at will during meditation for extended periods of time. At this point, methods and techniques are useless and absolute concentration is the most powerful way to progress further.

The Origin of OM – As Received from Guru Ashotosh

The most sacred sound in all of mantra practice is 'OM'. It is practiced widely throughout Asia, but most notably in the Himalayas, including India, Tibet, and Nepal. Some will say that OM is the most sacred sound, claiming it to be the name of God, a vibration of the supreme. But where does OM come from? How was OM discovered?

The answer to this question lies in the breath. While breathing, the in-breath creates the sound of AUH and the out-breath creates the sound HUM. When a master enters the Samadhi state, a state of silence beyond the duality of the mind, they no longer perceive a separation between the two sounds produced by the in-breath and the out-breath. As a result, the practitioner only hears constant repetitions of the sound OM, OM, OM. It was from this transcendental observation that OM was discovered.

The Daoists

The Daoists have gone to extensive lengths in the field of energy cultivation—entire series of books are dedicated to their various methods and practices. The most popular techniques focus on clearing the meridians (Microcosmic Orbit, Macrocosmic Orbit), visualization, awareness meditation, and cultivating the lower dan tien.

Lower Dan Tien Breathing

The lower dan tien is a central aspect when it comes to Daoist cultivation because it is the source of strength and power behind the kundalini energy that flows through the sacred disks. In this respect, the lower dan tien is like the engine inside of a car. By utilizing breathing techniques focused exclusively on the lower dan tien, it becomes possible to cultivate sexual energy faster.

Considering the life-force energy is contained in the air around one's self, lower dan tien training involves isolating the breathing exclusively to the lower stomach. Through this practice, one is filling the dan tien with vital energy (jing) at a faster pace. During the practice, the individual is doing isolation breathing by only moving the lower part of their stomach, and through doing so they are isolating the vital energy into the LDT area.

Lower dan tien breathing is only a temporary practice, and it is both mastered and completed when the practitioner begins to feel heat in the lower stomach while doing the exercise. The heat is by no means a bad thing, however, it is a warning sign from the body that the lower dan tien is sufficiently cultivated. After this point, further practice could potentially become dangerous for one's health.

When full, the jing inside of the lower dan tien creates friction when moving around as a result of the exercise, and this occurrence is expressed as heat. By pumping the lower stomach muscles in and out, one will be able to feel the heat generated from the friction caused by the energy inside of the lower dan tien.

Lower dan tien breathing serves the purpose of directly creating a foundation for newer practitioners. When practicing awareness meditation in a relaxed manner, one may notice that their breath naturally fills all three sections of the lungs. This is "natural breath" and is the ultimate form of breathing because it balances the psychological state. The lower portion of the lungs is correlated with physicality, middle portion with emotions, and upper portion with intellect.[3] Natural breathing creates a balance between all three.

Dan tien breathing can almost be considered opposite from mantra practice. Where mantras are focused towards purifying and awakening the sacred disks (the amplifiers of concentration), lower dan tien breathing is focused towards filling the lower dan tien (the battery/power source). Each practice by themselves is not a sufficient stand-alone practice. However, when combining mantra practice with lower dan tien breathing, the individual is both purifying the central channel and strengthening the force that rises through it. In Neidan training, Daoists will generally combine meditative concentration-based practice with LTD breathing in order to raise the sexual energy that was accumulated through LTD breathing practice.

Horse Stance

The horse stance is an alchemical technique that is popular with both energy cultivators and martial artists. This technique not only helps one master his/her body, but also increases the power of the lower dan tien. The great master Bhodidharma was very upset when he visited the temples in China and saw the monks hunching over scrolls. He went on to teach his disciples that meditation was not enough, and they also needed to train physically in order to ascend towards enlightenment. It is important to cultivate life when cultivating essence. This is where the horse stance comes in. Overall, from both a physical and energetic perspective, the horse stance can be viewed as an amplified foundation-building exercise.

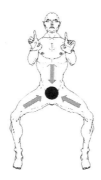

The Chinese refer to a correct horse stance posture as having "dawn." The practitioner should not be drooping or focusing all of the effort on the legs to hold the posture. Instead, to achieve "dawn," the focus of the posture should be centered at the core. The exercise will strengthen the legs, but not all of the focus is on the legs so a person with correct "dawn" is both stable and solid.

On a physical level, horse stance training works to strengthen the body by strengthening the legs. Leg strength is connected with testosterone, so with powerful legs the muscle mass of the entire body increases at an accelerated pace.

From an energetic perspective, by training with the horse stance posture the practitioner is cultivating and concentrating vital energy (jing) into the lower dan tien. This increases the speed that the lower dan tien is developed, and augments the individual's level of vitality. By working with the lower dan tien, the horse stance posture is also accelerating the ascension process by strengthening the kundalini and increasing the speed of kundalini rising.

Egyptian Methods

Ancient Egyptian methods are similar to the Daoist methods except with a powerful twist. The Egyptian methods utilize focused breathing, but they also combine it with visualization practice. When considering the breath, the air that is being inhaled contains chi/prana, or what some western researchers refer to as "Vitality Globules." The Vitality Globules in the air have seven different frequencies represented by the different colors of the visible light spectrum, and when the practitioner breathes in, the different frequencies of the vitality globules attach to a respective major energy center (according to frequency). However, if the individual utilizes visualization, they can actually alter the frequency of the vitality globules being inhaled, similar to a filter. Once this is done, the vital energy can be focused to develop a specific part of the etheric body. So by utilizing the breathing methods they are accumulating the vital energy in one location of the body, but by also using visualization they are altering the energy in order to increase the potency of the energy accumulated. The visualization practices utilized in many of the Western Hermetic practices are based on Egyptian methods.

An extraordinary account of the ancient Egyptian methods was discovered and circulated through the writings of a travelling antique dealer by the name of Count Stefan Colonna Walewski. Walewski was spending his time traveling in remote areas near Egypt and made contact with a group of indigenous people. He took an interest in these people and was actually taken in by them. What is interesting about these people is that they had special techniques that they would practice daily in order to reach an "immortal state."

"A stage of the saint. Expansion of the I, the ego, overlaps the bounds of the flesh, Ego becomes the outside, while the body becomes the seed on the inside. This is immortality, the way of the Gods. Ego grasps things unheard of and unimagined by the uninitiated, it is the stage of masters and saviors, bent on solving the karma of nations and races on this earth."

—Count Stefan Walewski[4]

During his stay, Walewski began to practice with the indigenous people and learned that the methods and techniques that he was being taught originated from the ancient Egyptians. Walewski recorded the techniques and wisdom that they presented him in his personal journal, which he eventually brought back with him and published for others to view. Today, most of Walewski's training and learning is detailed in *A System of Caucasian Yoga*, which is widely available. Since its publishing, many have trained the methods and techniques provided by Walewski. The text has been most notably accredited to the extraordinary healings surrounding Ruben Pipian, who actually learned of the system firsthand through a medicine man that apparently healed his seriously ill mother by only waving his hands across her body a few times.

The Egyptian methods involve four separate intervals of seven second breathing. The seven second breathing is important because this rate matches the natural rhythm of the Earth.[5] For this reason, seven second breathing is known as "Master Breath." The Egyptian techniques combine visualization with breathing, which is a middle ground between the Indian methods and the Daoist methods.

The idea behind the Egyptian methods is that the different sections of the lungs have subtle colors associated with them relating to an individual's physiology. Besides the sections of the lungs, each color also associates with a section of the head. When looking at the lungs, the lower section represents the physical, the middle section is the emotional, and the upper section is the mental. Personally, I find it very relevant. The heart is near the middle section of the lungs and is commonly associated with emotions. Additionally, if one observes people that are always thinking, they are usually only breathing from the top section of their lungs (associated with yellow), these people's foreheads also become very hot. I have worked as an accountant and noticed the effects in myself. The lower section of the lungs is red and is associated with the physical. This is relevant to Daoist alchemy as it equates with the jing vitality.

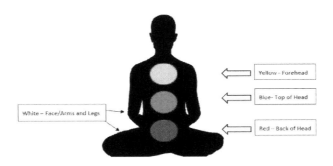

To give a brief summary, the Egyptian methods involve isolating the breathing to one section of the lungs at a time. This is similar to the Daoist breathing, however it utilizes all sections of the lungs equally. The breath intervals are seven seconds in, one second hold, and then seven seconds out. One visualizes breathing in the color that is associated with the current section of the lungs, and then visualizes charging that section of the lungs with the specific color while breathing out. After one has breathed in, hold, and out, they move onto the next section of the lungs. The fourth breath interval is the white breath, and it is associated with the face, arms, and legs. A total of three sets are completed each day, twice a day, with 30 seconds between each set.[6]

Personally, I believe that these methods are very relevant and potent. They are known as the "short path," which is a term commonly used by the Tibetans to refer to a practice of purifying the central channel through techniques in a quick and direct way. It is common to feel vibrations and heat while practicing these methods.

Chastity

"Be sober, diligent, and chaste; avoid all wrath. In public or in secret ne'er permit thou any evil; and above all else respect thyself."

–Pythagoras

Throughout many yogic, hermetic, spiritual, and religious organizations, a varying degree of emphasis has been placed on sex and the practice of chastity.

"The power of illusion acts in man particularly by means of his sexual center, or more exactly at its expense.

–Boris Mouravieff[7]

Considering that the sexual energy is utilized in order to purify the central channel, its depletion hinders this process. The abuse of the sexual center, increases the power of illusion: a mental fog, similar to a lack of intelligence.

"Celibacy is to a Yogi what electricity is to an electric bulb. It is the only key to open the Sushumna (the chief among astral tubes in the human body running inside the spinal column) and awaken the kundalini (the primordial cosmic energy located in the individual). The generative energy, which, when we are loose, dissipates and makes us unclean, when we are continent invigorates and inspires us. Chastity is the flowering of man; and what are called Genius, Heroism, Holiness, and the like, are but various fruits which succeed it."

–Henry David Thoreau[8]

Through sexual abuse, the individual is regularly depleted of jing, sexual energy, thus hindering the process of alchemy. After intercourse, the body goes into a recovery mode for approximately 72-hours where the lower dan tien becomes isolated.[9] This period varies based on one's physical condition and age. Men may notice that if they attempt strenuous exercise after having intercourse they will cramp and feel pain in the area of the lower dan tien. This is because the dan tien, associated with the physical body, has become isolated, but the body needs an energy source.

While the sexual energy plays an important role in alchemy, and should not be abused, intercourse actually clears the nervous system, helping a person maintain a regulated mental state. In other words, to avoid intercourse for too long can cause a person to go crazy. Realizing this, the concept of rejecting impure sexuality and that of seeking "soul-mate" has emerged—a form of pure sexuality based on love that is in harmony with the realization of one's true nature.

Vegetarianism

Ashrams and temples often adhere to strict dietary regiments centered around vegetarianism. The function behind vegetarianism in relation to yoga, is that it keeps one's concentration raised and reduces sexual urges. Meat is a dense food that slows a person down, physically inducing tiredness and mentally reducing concentration. People that want to constantly stay at high levels of concentration eat very clean foods avoiding meat. When living in Mt. Shasta we would call the practice of vegetarianism eating "alien food," because just by avoiding meat and being on the mountain we were experiencing shifts in our mental state. Most people in the Western world have actually become desensitized to the effects of meat, because they eat it so consistently that they are not aware of its effects on the body: similar to how many people have become desensitized to the taste of clean water.

Different degrees of vegetarianism actually occur naturally as an individual's intelligence increases. As one's concentration intensifies, they require less dense foods, such as meat, and still remain sufficiently healthy. Similar to cultivating the etheric body, these individuals are receiving nutrition from a different dimension of themselves. In the end, training one's concentration is the central focus and dietary fluctuations begin to happen naturally as the spirit is developed.

Actively transitioning into a vegetarian diet takes time, especially for the average American; it took me about two years until I was comfortable. Visiting countries like India make it easy, as a majority of their food is vegetarian, albeit being extremely dairy based. For those interested, the practice is to adapt to the vegetarian diet slowly by preferring chicken over any other type of meat and also avoiding pastas. Indian yogis have very specific dietary guidelines when it comes to yogic/meditation practices, I recommend Kundalini Yoga by Swami Sivananda for more information. The downside to forced vegetarianism, however, is that it can weaken one's body, the source of will power.

FAKING YOUR SECURITY

Only fools and saints are truly and absolutely secure about themselves.

Only an absolute fool can be so ignorant of the way of the universe that he feels secured in his bliss fool ignorant self.

Today, in our present society, it's vital to exhibit only your sense of self confidence.

It's a delight to watch people who are absolutely secure with themselves.

However, the greatest secret is, the rest of the world is faking.

It is to different degrees, and some are better fakers than others.

You and I know that we will not have found true security within us until we've touched our soul and spirit

In the meantime, we are to a different degree faking our security.

Don't try too hard.
Be practical and realistic.

We're still existing in this mortal world.
And we must learn to live both as spirit as well as human.

Enlightenment is for those who can understand and live as both in heaven as it is on earth, and on earth as it is in heaven.

-Tian De

THE REMNANTS OF ALCHEMY
[Death and Rebirth]

When examining the cycle of death and rebirth, specific information has been recorded by different groups of investigators around the world. The Tibetan monks in particular have recorded detailed information regarding death and rebirth in their famous text *The Bardo Thodol (The Tibetan Book of the Dead)*. According to *The Bardo Thodol*, after the death of the physical body, a deceased person's soul exists in "the bardo" for 49 days until it is reincarnated into another body. Therefore, the bardo can be seen as the transition stage between death and rebirth. During the 49 days spent in the bardo, the soul experiences many phenomena based on past lives, and depending on how the soul navigates through these phenomenon determines one's situation in future lives.[1]

The first stage of the Tibetan Bardo supervening the death of the physical body is the "Chikhai" Bardo, which is comprised of psychic happenings at moment of death. These psychic happenings are important because they give insight into the character of the individual's next incarnation. At the moment of death, the individual enters into an altered state of awareness, and from this conscious state they gain a full understanding of the path in front of them. Often times, the look on an individual's face at this moment can indicate the positive or negative nature of the path awaiting them.[2]

The next phase is the "Chonyid" Bardo, which is a dream state that supervenes immediately after the death of the physical body causing one to experience what are called "karmic illusions."[3] These illusions can be either good or bad, and are attributed to how a person lived during their life.

John Chang, an experienced meditation practitioner native to Indonesia, expands on this phenomenon in detail. He explains how after the death of the physical body most people will enter into either a "white wave" or a "black wave" depending upon their actions/karma. He describes the "waves" as actual etheric, or non-physical, locations in the sky. The "white wave" is a place where those in positive karmic alignment reside and receive anything they ask for. John Chang describes this place as a type of heaven, but very much an illusory heaven and not authentic. The "black wave" is described by Chang as a place where everyone is in a state of suffering, making it a most horrible place. However, similar to the Tibetan tradition, John Chang insists that the black wave and the white wave are complete illusion and that all the souls will return to the same place after a certain amount of time spent in the respective wave. Because it is illusion, the beings in the black wave and white wave are unaware of the true nature of their surroundings and are residing in a state of ignorance. Similar to the Tibetan Chikhai Bardo, before death, Chang also mentions that a person will get a glimpse of what lies in store for them, and the look on their face at the moment of death can be an indication of whether they will go to the "white wave" or the "black wave."[4]

(After the death of the physical body when the pulse stops and the breath stops, the body is still warm. The person is not actually dead, they are in a state of dreaming. These dreams are explained to be influenced by how they lived, they are karmic visions believed to influence one's next life.)

The Tibetans explain that after the stage of "karmic illusions," one goes into the final stage of bardo, which is referred to as "Sidpa" Bardo. This is a state where the soul begins preparation for rebirth, but more importantly, the Tibetans insist that there is a possibility of attaining realization and enlightenment at this stage.[5] However, if enlightenment is not attained, then the individual will fall prey to sexual fantasies and become caught by the womb. It is believed that during this stage of Bardo, the different wombs appear as enticing illusions that the souls can become sidetracked by on their path of light. The wombs can appear as glorious palaces offering large meals and beautiful women, but only lead to rebirth.

(This stage of bardo is emulated in Toei Animation's popular television show *Dragon Ball Z* after the main character, Goku, dies in battle with Raditz. After his death, Goku is sent to travel along "Snake Way," a long winding pathway that is a representation of the "path of light," but along the way he is sidetracked by Princess Snake. She lures him into her castle and treats him as a royal guest offering him food and beautiful women. However, Goku eventually "sees" through the illusion and realizes that the princess is actually a giant snake in disguise trying to devour him! The entire illusion of the castle that Goku entered was her stomach (womb). Goku was actually inside of her. However, he eventually breaks free from the illusion and manages to escape her stomach and get back onto Snake Way—Goku was able to overcome the enticing womb of rebirth that the Tibetans describe, continuing his journey.)

The Arhats, or humans who have attained enlightenment while on earth, follow a different path after the death of the physical body. In the above quote, Tian De mentions that the beings who become "one" with the universe, operate in the "Universal Body" after death, which is a state of consciousness outside of the continuous cycle of death and rebirth. Looking at other texts, it becomes apparent that after the death of the physical body, these beings consciously follow a continuous trail of light, similar to Snake Way.[6]

The Shen Double

A common occurrence when researching spiritual development is the ability of an individual to create one or multiple clones of themselves. Many are familiar with the "etheric double" from the Egyptians, however, this phenomenon is also noted by the Tibetans,[7] and is referred to as the "shen double" by the Daoists, and bilocation or doppelganger in Western traditions. A quick search of "bilocation" will show that the phenomenon of physical clones has appeared in early Greek philosophy, shamanism, paganism, occultism, Hinduism (as one of the siddhis), theosophy, Christian mysticism, and Jewish mysticism.[8]

The Immortal Fetus[9]

In Daoism, the shen double is grown and matured during a stage known as the "immortal fetus," a stage that one reaches after attaining "light body" or enlightenment. Similar to the immortal fetus, this child that is grown and developed in the lower stomach is referred to as the Infans Solaris (literally meaning "Sun Child") in Hermeticism and Gnosticism. The idea is that with time, the "child" grows into a separate clone of one's self that can travel throughout the world, gaining information and impressions.

"The yin spirit is like an infant: first it is slowly nurtured and developed inside the abdomen; then it is transferred to the nirvana chamber in the brain. When projection of spirit is first practiced, it is only made to act in the immediate vicinity, and it is recalled very quickly. After long-term training, when the yin spirit has become powerful and can enter and exit freely, then it can be allowed to travel a bit further, and it can be projected several times in a day. Because it is the traveling of vitality, energy, and spirit, after this capacity has been developed it travels as fast as the speed of thought itself. By different uses of vitality, energy, and spirit, it is possible to manifest form or not manifest form; herein lies the secret of the "art of reproducing the body"."

-Wang Liping[10]

Some believe that Jesus Christ used a yogic technique to stop his breathing in order to die on the cross, but remain alive. However, considering the possibility of bi-location, it would seem more apparent that he was instead using a shen double.[11] With the possibility of being in two locations at once, the body that was being tortured to death was not actually his true body.

Daoist teacher Wang Liping explains that the capacity of the three dan tiens is what determines the physicality of the double.[12] In the west, Daskalos, one who has personally described his ability to perform bilocation, explains that it is possible to materialize different aspects of the body at will: he uses his hand as an example.[13]

Multiple Doubles[14]

In Daoism, after the "shen double" has fully developed, it begins a process of splitting into multiple clones. These multiple bodies allow the practitioner to maintain awareness in multiple locations around the world simultaneously. In *The Magus of Java*, John Chang explained how his teacher would always know whether or not he had trained on a certain day, because his teacher observed him like a God.[15]

DESTINY

Everything in us depends on the goal we set for ourselves.

What we want to achieve.

Or in other words, our destiny.

As you desire, so is your decision.

As you decide, so are your deeds.

As are your deeds, so is your destiny.

Man is the architect of his successes and failures.

"Heaven propose. Man dispose."

A painter who does not make the colors of his own aura more beautiful is no painter.

A musician who cannot tune himself, his heart, and his mind will know nothing about harmony.

A sculptor with all twisted, deformed, and unlighted spirit knows nothing about forms.

A writer who writes the words with voices in their ear that no one hears, within the sound of Silence, knows about the splendors of inspirations from without in his work.

A true painter, a true sculptor, poet or writer, sage or mystic, aspirant or initiate, works on his inner self within, the ideal work that is all beauty and all splendors.

A human being whom has become a living masterpiece and who writes the book of Himself, does more for mankind than all the libraries, museums, and works of art in the world for they are Dead, and he is Alive.

-Tian De

RANKINGS OF CONSCIOUSNESS
[Observing the Ascent]

As discussed previously, while following the light of consciousness the entire existence of an individual is *evolving*. Through observation, different alchemical lineages have created classifications of man in order to rank an individual's evolution. These are specific class based rankings that are used to organize people based on how evolved they are. The lineages are considering elements of one's being beyond the physical, and analyzing the subtle qualities of man associated with spiritual evolution.

Ascension in Daoist Alchemy

The most comprehensive ranking system for human evolution is the immortal classifications created by the Daoist alchemists. This ranking system pin-points specific "graduations" or developments along one's development and the qualities associated with each stage of evolution.

According to Daoist alchemy, humans fall into one of five distinct evolutionary categories: Ghost Immortal, Human Immortal, Earth Immortal, Spiritual Immortal, and Celestial Immortal. All of the classifications are considered immortals because the Daoist alchemists recognize that the inner soul awareness endures beyond the death of the physical body. This is consistent with the idea of reincarnation. The awareness within each sentient being is immortal, carrying all the memories and experiences of every lifetime. However, not all of the Daoist evolutionary stages consider one as a "true immortal," because in many of these levels the individual does not retain conscious awareness throughout their various journeys between bodies. They are in a sense drifting through continual rebirth. The awareness may be immortal, but the being is still asleep in a sense and harboring dormant potential.

Gui Xian (Ghost Immortal)

Gui Xian is the lowest level of achievement. The Ghost Immortal most closely resembles the living dead, they are caught in the material realm knowing nothing of spirit, the unformed, where they came from and return. While alive in human form these immortals most closely resemble the animal class, as they are primarily concerned with food, sex, and shelter. Ghost Immortals are not free thinkers they must be told what to do this is why they are possessed by others thoughts and beliefs.

Ghost immortals control themselves in reincarnation but since they enter the ghost gates with no first and last name they cannot enter the Bonlai (Daoist magical islands).[1] After death, this class of individual is confined to the continuous cycle of death and rebirth.

Ren Xian (Human Immortal)

At the human immortal level, one has activated the pairing of Kan and Li, which is the heart fire and kidney water.

The prevalent quality of Ren Xian is that they endure a long human lifespan. For the human immortal, the body is stronger and develops resistance to external pathogens preventing them from causing illness, and as a result, these individuals remain healthy with little sickness.[2] An estimated one in ten humans are at the Ren Xian level.

While not directly acknowledged by the Daoists this stage is achieved when one opens the heart chakra and activates the fourth chakra circuit.

Di Xian (Earth Immortal)

Earth immortal is marked by the fusion of yin and yang chi inside of the cranium. This fusion marks the birth of Houtian Qi, also known as Electric Qi. As a result, this level of practitioner is considered to have supernatural powers to a slight extent. Practitioners at this level also develop a further degree of resistance towards sickness, only becoming sick on rare occasions.

After the death of the physical body, a practitioner at this level does not leave the earth, and are still dependent on the earth's energies to survive. Earth Immortals are not however free from continual rebirth and eventually reincarnate.

While not directly acknowledged by the Daoists this is stage is reached when one opens the sixth chakra.

Shen Xian (Spirit Immortal)

At this stage, the three yangs (jing, chi, and shen) gather at the crown of the head.[3] The joining of the three yangs births the creation of Ling, which is referred to by some as Xian Tian qi or golden wave energy. Yin totally disappears and one becomes pure yang, returning to the three mountains of Tao.[4] Earlier in the meditation section a quote from the Golden Flower explained how through the awareness the individual was going beyond the "dregs of yin." The pure conscious awareness reached at Shen Xian level is of pure yang, the individual is beyond all dregs of yin nature (lack of freedom created by the mind). The pure yang awareness at this stage is commonly equated with "enlightenment."

The human body is emptied and the Xian Fetus is created. After the immortal fetus develops, the yang spirit is able to consciously enter in and out of the fontanel (soft spot on top of head) and can travel anywhere in the universe. The yang spirit leaves out of the top of the human head and the adept born into the spiritual world (sainthood).

Following further development, the yang spirit begins to multiply, creating doubles. The number of doubles gradually grows over time, allowing the practitioner to be fully conscious in various different locations (sometimes more than seven places), and receive impressions from all these places simultaneously.[5]

The Spiritual Immortal is the first true class of immortal, because these beings are free from the perpetual cycle of death and rebirth and consciously follow a stream of light after the death of the physical body.[6]

Tian Xian (Celestial Immortal)

The final achievement of conscious evolution in Daoist Alchemy is that of the Celestial Immortal. Attaining the celestial immortal status is said to take nearly ten years in absolute meditation.[7] This stage of development is centered around achieving complete integration of the physical body with the light of the spirit.

Even though fully integrated with the light of the spirit, masters at this level are still limited to a human life span (Bhodidharma lived 200 years.[8] However, after death, the physical body completely dissolves into the light of the spirit leaving nothing remaining. This is similar to George Lucas's *Star Wars* where Darth Vader strikes down Obi-Wan Kenobi, but instead of falling to the ground, his body disappears completely. This occurrence, however, is not unique to the Daoists. It is said to have been displayed by Jesus. He completely merged his physical body with the light of his spirit on Mount Tabor in order to endure the crucifixion and be able to resurrect and dematerialize himself.[9] Similarly, many state that when the grave of the great master Bodhidharma was opened, only his shoe remained. The great Tibetan master, Padmasambhava, was also recorded to have spontaneously burst into light at the end of his life. After the death of the physical body, a celestial immortal master can materialize anywhere on Earth at will.[10]

EASTERN CHRISTIANITY
[The Royal Way]

Rankings regarding the ascent of man towards greater reaches of consciousness can also be found when looking at traditional Eastern Orthodoxy. These rankings have historically been referred to as the "Royal Way." An individual's ascent/evolution towards God is divided into seven distinct levels: the seven levels of man. These stages have been notably expounded upon and popularized through the works of George Gurdjieff, Boris Mouravieff, and P.D. Ouspensky.

Man 1, 2, and 3

The first three levels of man, known as man one, two, and three, are all considered to be on the same evolutionary level, and equal in ranking. It believed that the majority of humans fall into these three categories.

That which determines one's placement with regards to man one, two, and three, is not so much evolution but instead one's conscious alignment/disposition with relation to their physical, emotional, and intellectual (mental) centers. Man one is mostly centered in the physical, man two in the emotional, and man three in the intellectual (or mental).

Man 1. Physical Man	During the first three stages, the individual has no conscious direction and is being pulled in different directions by their uncontrollable emotions and thoughts.
Man 2. Emotional Man	
Man 3. Intellectual Man	

While man one, two, and three are aligned to one of the three centers they are still in a fog and constantly being displaced by the other two centers. They are noted to be unstable and in a state of constantly changing illogically with themselves.[1] They are considered to be "lost in the wilderness," so to speak.

Trial by Fire

The process of evolving beyond man one, two, and three is known as the "Trial by Fire." The idea is that through increased tension surrounding an individual, it eventually causes them to become consciously centered. An analogy used to describe this process is taking an array of metal pieces and heating them all up. The heat causes the pieces to slowly mold together, and as a result, the "magnetic center" of the individual is created.[2] The individual is divided at first between the emotional, physical, and mental centers, but then they slowly gain control of themselves.

The "magnetic center" is best described as a habitual level of thought that helps guide one in a specific direction, despite the hundreds of different pieces of the psyche working against each other. This allows one to develop in a particular direction, instead of randomly, like looking for something in the dark.[3]

Over time as the individual continually identifies with the magnetic center, the center begins to grow and take shape. When the magnetic center is fully developed, the individual gains complete authority over the lower three centers.[4] The individual becomes man four. At this stage one brings with them a degree of centeredness regardless of the external situation that they are placed in. It is from this level that one begins the true work and natural self-observation.

Note: Besides gaining authority over the three lower centers, there is also a notion that these centers grow and develop—a notion of cultivation. A connection can be seen when considering the ancient Egyptian methods discussed previously that would use focused breathing and visualization in order to cultivate three distinct energy centers. These centers are primarily the lower stomach (physical), solar plexus (emotional), and upper chest (intellectual). One could almost say that these techniques are the alchemical side behind Eastern Orthodox evolution. With this being considered, then man four would represent the sixth chakra fusion. Sixth chakra fusion is only mastered once the centers below it (representing physical, emotional, and intellectual) are cultivated.

As one continues to develop and equalize the three lower centers, as a result of residing in the magnetic center, one begins to form a connection with what is referred to as the "higher emotional center." It is through this connection with the higher emotional center that one is able to progress towards man five. The reason that the emotional center is able to help one progress forward is because it is the only body[5] ever truly sure of anything. It feels, and it doesn't think. It is sure of its feelings, while the intellect can find just as many reasons for as against anything.

Man 5

As this development is continuing, the magnetic center identifies itself more and more with the higher emotional center. When the three lower centers are fully developed and equilibrated, the magnetic center then fully identifies with the higher emotional center.[6] It is from the complete communion with the higher emotional center that one reaches the attainment of man five.

Those at this level reach what is known as the "second rebirth." At this stage one's personality is refined into the individuality. Man five is permanently conscious of his real "I".[7] (This can be equated with the pure-yang Daoist Spiritual Immortal) They are awakened, and abide in the conscious state that is known as enlightenment in most systems. Man five is also noted to acquire new faculties and powers.

Man 6

Man six gains communion with what is known as the higher intellectual center. At this stage one develops the supernatural faculties thus acquired previously to their utmost limits. Man six is noted to be virtually superhuman.

Note: It is important to clarify the information presented up to this point. There is no higher physical body in the Gnostic system. Only the emotional center has direct connection with its higher center/body (the higher emotional center). Therefore, the intellect cannot commune with the ultimate intellect, God, without first communing with the higher emotional body through the lower emotional body. So, it is like climbing up a ladder.

Man 7

Man seven marks a permanent attainment. What is different about man one through six is that they can lose everything and revert backwards if they are not treading carefully. However, once man seven is attained there is no going back. Man seven is so advanced that they have to shed their physical form in order to evolve further.[8] It is believed that at this stage one travels to the Sun after the death of the physical body, where there is a celestial heaven.

Note: The distinction that one can revert to back down to lower state of evolution after having attained man five (associated with second rebirth / enlightenment) is an important distinction that is not commonly acknowledged. This is similar to the story of King Solomon, the son of King David, who was once enlightened but fell due to his obsession with women, and his Temple fell down, with his treasure inside, losing his enlightenment.

Means of Spiritual Progression

Besides the different levels of man in Eastern Orthodoxy that represent one's spiritual progression, there are also descriptions of the different routes/means towards spiritual progression. There are generally five different routes that have been specified that can take one higher up the evolutionary ladder. All of these paths prepare one's "house" so that the master (super-conscious awareness) can arrive. The house is a combination of the physical, emotional, and intellectual centers of an individual.

The first way, is the path of the "fakir." The fakir is someone who seeks to submit their physical body to God, and this is generally done though physical pain. They work on the first room of their "house." One can cultivate their physical body through physical activity such as working out or martial arts. However, when considering extremes, this path is also very similar those like the "Ice Man" who submits himself to freezing temperatures, and also the ancient yogis who would painfully hang themselves from trees.

The second way, is the way of the monk. This is generally seen as someone who submits their emotional body to God. It is often times a "fear of God." It is an idea that is expressed in the Old Testament often. This man works on the second room in his house.

The third way is the way of the yogi. The yogi is someone who seeks to submit their intellectual body to God. He works on the third room in his house. The third way is for someone who seeks to submit their intellectual body to God.

Each of these three are considered to be a quicker means of evolution than the previous. However, George Gurdjieff presents the fourth way which is a concept of working on all three rooms simultaneously in order to ready the house as quickly as possible for the Master to arrive—the awakened self. Therefore, the fourth way is seen as an even faster method of progression.

Boris Mouravieff later presented the "fifth way" with his application of the Royal Way. This path focuses heavily upon the idea of "soulmates:" two individuals that are destined to meet each other and assist each other towards enlightenment. Mouravieff explains that the true "I" of an individual is bipolar, encompassing both male and female attributes.[9] It is because the true state of one's being is both male and female that when an individual meets their "polar opposite" they embody a natural state of completion/balance that helps to guide them towards reaching their full potential.

Silence will then be the depository of the fullness of his love.

–The Golden Book[10]

An experiential state of silence is the result of interaction between two soulmates. Boris Mouravieff also explained that soulmates are destined to meet at least once in their lifetimes.[11]

The Five Eyes of Buddha

As mentioned previously, the Buddha once explained to his disciple Ananda that beings on different levels, although they may look at the same thing, will actually see each thing according to their own perspective. In Buddhism, the various forms in this world are perceived from five different levels, and each person has a different level of perception according to their level of development with regards to awakening the "Five Eyes."[1] The manifestation of the five different levels of perception are represented by the awakening of the Flesh Eye, Heavenly Eye, Wisdom Eye, Dharma Eye, and the Buddha Eye.[2]

Each consecutive eye represents an experiential attainment on the path of evolution, a shift like a new layer of reality becoming illuminated. When new types of light can be perceived, the individual becomes conscious of additional possibilities.

The Buddhists, however, are not describing the eyes simply as a metaphor in order to make a distinction between the different layers of perception, but the eyes are instead real components of one's subtle body. Each of the five eyes are a dormant potential that naturally awakens in a consecutive fashion during one's conscious evolution, bringing along a new level of perception and understanding. These psychic eyes are subtle and of the etheric body, however, once awakened, their existence is so distinct to the practitioner that they actually feel physical.

Awakening the subtle eyes is also associated with perceiving beyond the limitations of ordinary "matter" and walking into the "extrasensory." Normally, one can only perceive a small range of visible phenomenon known as the "visible light spectrum" (wavelengths from about 390 nm to 700 nm). However, those who meditate are often rumored with being able to perceive beyond the boundaries of the ordinary senses. When studying the Five Eyes in particular, many will find themselves reading about seeing through walls, perceiving sickness in others, or even viewing distant planets.

The following is a description of each of the Five Eyes of Buddha. Under special permission, also included are descriptions provided by Master Sheng Yen.[3]

The Flesh Eye

Many are already well-acquainted with the flesh eye. This is the experiential perception of ordinary people, and refers to the physical eyes of the flesh that sentient beings are born with. The flesh eye distinguishes color and form. These eyes operate in the visible light spectrum seeing the physical, and because of this, the vision of the flesh eye can become blocked by other physical objects, such as simply putting up a piece of paper. The flesh eye is considered the least powerful of the five eyes.

"This eye is quite limited. You can't see things that are too big, too small, too far, and too close. The fleshy eye is so weak that it is almost useless."

–Sheng Yen

The Heavenly Eye

The second eye to awaken is known as the "heavenly eye." This subtle eye is able to perceive beyond the range of the visible light spectrum that encompass the flesh eyes. Because of this expansion, the heavenly eye is able to perceive in darkness, at long distances, and also through physical obstructions.[4]

There exist stories of the Buddha training his disciples, and helping them to develop the psychic eyes through meditation. In one story, Buddha's disciple Anirudha actually loses his vision from practicing continuous meditation with his eyes open. The Buddha, however, tells Anirudha that the human eyes are of no value and that there are better eyes to acquire. Through further training, Anirudha was able to develop the heavenly eye, which allowed his vision to become truly vast.[5] The story goes that through this development, Anirudha was able to overcome his loss of sight and gain higher more expansive vision.

The heavenly eye is sometimes referred to as the "God eye," because it is attributed with being able to see anything, anywhere. Previously, it was mentioned how the yogi, instead of observing reality through a telescope, actually evolves their own experiential awareness/perception in order to gain a more comprehensive understanding of reality. However, through the use of the heavenly eye, the yogi is said to also be able to observe phenomenon at the molecular level as well as far off into the cosmos and space. So in this regard, the heavenly eye can be compared with both a microscope and a telescope.[6]

Today, when looking at the estimated five-thousand-year-old Sumerian tablets, many people wonder how these ancient people were able to map the entire solar system. However, through the awakening of the heavenly eye, it could be possible to study astronomy in great detail.[7] It would follow that these ancients were able to tap into their inner potential and awaken their ability to study distant stars without the use of external technology.

As the heavenly eye's perception with regards to distant objects is not only limited to the physical frequency, it is also said to be even capable of witnessing events taking place in the thirty-three heavens.[8] For example, it is said that the heavenly eye can perceive the gods themselves dining or sitting in meditation.[9]

The Wisdom Eye

The third level of perception is the "wisdom eye," also known as the "arhat eye." Those at this level of perception are Buddhas, or awakened ones, who have attained a conscious state beyond death and rebirth.

Those at the previous two levels of perception associated with the flesh eye and the heavenly eye still have vexations. This eye, however, is known as the wisdom eye because the individual has truly attained wisdom (an experiential *quality*), having lost the conceptual sense of self and eliminated all vexations.

"The sutra says that when an arhat (wisdom eye) observes this world, he sees it the same way an ordinary being sees a mango in his hand, and he sees it with complete clarity. He can not only see this world, but he can see a great chilocosm[10] of worlds. Why is his vision so vast? He no longer has a sense of self, therefore the chilocosm is there before him, unobstructed by his own perceptions or interests."

–Sheng Yen

From this clarity, those with the wisdom eye are able to experientially perceive the connected nature of all things. That nothing has an independent existence of its own and that all phenomena are non-substantial.[11] Those with the wisdom eye are also attributed to no longer having a fear even death.

The Dharma Eye

The fourth level of perception is the "dharma eye," also known as the "bodhisattva eye."

168

"Why is this eye, and not that of the arhat, called the dharma eye? Even though the arhat has liberated himself from self, or ego, there is still a sense of discrimination between the realms of birth and death. But for the bodhisattva there is neither birth nor death, samsara nor nirvana. He has no attachment to the Dharma[12], and thus he has the dharma eye."

–Sheng Yen

Those who obtain the dharma eye reside in a conscious space where there is no longer separation between birth nor death, samsara, or nirvana. It is from this presence that those with the dharma eye experientially understand the illusory nature of suffering and do not perceive it as real. From this understanding compassion for other beings naturally arises.[13]

The dharma eye is also attributed with allowing one the ability to thoroughly investigate everything. While this includes a perceptual awareness into true nature of all of the teachings, it also pertains to seemingly supernatural investigations. This includes, for example, gaining the ability to use this eye in order to learn about past lives.[14]

The Buddha Eye – The Eye of Omniscience

The fifth level of perception is known as the "Buddha eye." What is fascinating about the Buddha eye is that its awakening further enhances the previous four eyes to their highest level. This brings a state of perception that cannot be comprehended with words, and must be experienced in order to gain a true grasp of the experience.

When described, opening the Buddha eye is like entering into a higher understanding of reality, one that transcends conventional understanding and perception. Visual phenomenon and ideas of far and near, large and small are transcended into a higher experiential understanding. Many refer to this eye as the "eye of omniscience" because from this state of transcendental understanding comes an all-knowing mindset.

When abiding in this state one perceives the true nature of life from a consciousness rooted beyond the past, present, and future.[15] This is the experiential quality of Entering the Infinite.

While all of the eyes feel real to the practitioner, the Buddha eye is the most distinct. It is located between the eyebrows, and may for a short time startle those who awaken it unknowingly.[16]

Retaining the Eyes

"The Buddha explained to Ananda that he must see into the true nature of things. In this way he will see his own true nature. This is what the Ch'an sect calls "seeing into your own true nature." But this can be somewhat misleading, because it might sound as if your true nature is something separate from yourself. That is not the case. Your true nature is your self; it is not apart from it."

–Sheng Yen

The "Five Eyes of Buddha" are dormant potentials that are a direct result of conscious evolution. They are connected to the entire system and activate in tandem with the etheric body. Understanding that they relate to the quality of "light" that is perceived, it becomes evident that when working to expand the awareness the individual is also awakening the five eyes. In Buddhism, retaining the eyes is connected with ideas of doing good deeds.

Ascension in Tibetan Buddhism

When the teachings of Buddhism were brought to Tibet they merged with the indigenous and ritualistic Bon tradition. This fusion came to form a unique fusion that is Tibetan Buddhism. Because of Bon's influence, Tibetan Buddhism is a very esoteric branch of Buddhism that is strongly focused on long periods of isolated meditation and mystical attainments. One of the more interesting aspects of the Tibetan society is the "Gomchen," a member whose role in society is to spend day and night in seated meditation. During this time, their duty is to capture stray demons in the society.[1]

The oldest school of Tibetan Buddhism is the Nyingma tradition (translated as: "ancient tradition"), which is founded based on the teachings of Padmasambhava: a high level meditation master recorded to have completely dissolved his physical body into light. At the core of the Nyingma tradition is "Dzogchen," which is also known as Ati Yoga or "Great Perfection."

Tibetan Buddhism - Realizing Dzogchen

With regards to spiritual development, the first attainment is to realize the state of Dzogchen. The state of Dzogchen is a realization of one's primordial nature: a realization of the true self. The state of one's being after attaining Dzogchen level realization is commonly compared to a mirror that reflects with complete openness but is not affected by the reflections. Accompanying this level of realization is also the ability to enter into the state of samadhi at will: a level of calmness compared with the death-like state.[2]

The practices associated with reaching Dzogchen realization are known as Trekchö. The Tibetans teach that one should experience realization by making a distinction between the true-mind and the false-mind. This is very similar to developing intelligence versus intellect. The Trekchö practice also involves forgiving and dissolving one's karma until it holds no cause.[3]

Rainbow Body Development - Embodying Cosmic Awareness

After realizing one's primordial nature, the next step is for the individual to merge with the universe—this is known as "developing the Rainbow Body." In Tibetan, the rainbow body of pure light is called "Ja-lus" and is translated as: "The Great Attainment." The practice focused towards developing the rainbow body of light is known as Tögal. This practice encourages one to transcend hope and fear and to remain present in the moment.[4]

The process of evolving the rainbow body and merging with the universe has three major stages, and the extent of one's development is commonly measured by observing the physical form after the practitioner's death.

When the practitioner dies at the first level of rainbow body, their body shrinks, sometimes to the size of a baby. This process occurs after one's death and is not preceded by any physical signs; it takes on average seven days for the body to shrink. The amount that the physical form shrinks is dependent on one's development, but it is said that usually a small, child-sized body remains.[5] This level of rainbow body achievement has been attributed to thousands of practitioners in Tibet. However, the legitimacy of this number is to be questioned because there are rivaling lineages. The book *Heart Drops of Dharmakaya: Dzogchen Practice of the Bon Tradition* is one example of an account regarding of this phenomenon.

In the West, to my understanding, the phenomenon of shrinking bodies is largely unheard of. Ordinarily, after the death of a person we bury the body, it is cremated, or it is sent to a laboratory.

The second stage of rainbow body attainment is recognized by the physical body dissolving into pure light at the time of death: only the hair and nails of the practitioner remain. During this process the body starts to shrink and shine, and sometimes float, until it reaches the size of a baby, and then the body completely disappears in a flash of bright light.[6]

The rarest and most advanced stage of the rainbow body is known as the "great transference." This level is a complete integration of the physical body with the rainbow body. At this stage, the practitioner not only completely dissolves the physical body into light, but remains functional and visible as light.[7] This stage has been commonly attributed to the Tibetan practitioner Padmasambhava, but I believe it was also attained by Jesus.

Rankings of Ascension in Perspective

All of the lineages are describing the path of spiritual evolution, and many of them have commonalities with three attainments: See the Light, Become the Light, and Merge with the Light.

See the Light = Activating the spirit, Sixth Chakra Awareness.

Become the Light = Realizing Primordial Nature, Light Body.

Merge with the Light = Complete physical Integration with the light of the spirit, merging with the universe or cosmic awareness.

Persevere for the Divine Within

If we wish to make any advancement or progress, we must erect our conscious being with strong will, a desire of unconditional love, and a pure mental synthesis of wisdom. This allows us to enamor ourselves against temptations of the lower basal and false nature that detour our lighthouse leading our way into the ocean of repeated birth and death.

It is our responsibility to construct a synthesis according to our own tendencies and affinities and have an aspiration to grow spiritually, embodying a true living luminous lifestyle—symbolically speaking, a representation of love and light.

Great masters in every age and ancient tradition teach us these simple truths.

It is through realizing one's Self, by learning and understanding oneself, that the supreme discovery that we and the source of our being, or we and the universe whom some refer to as God, are simultaneously "One and Different." That is when we realize that we are "One" in consciousness. The "One" is aware of our eternal position and relationship with the source within.

And the Different—the one who lives in sense gratification, indulgences, and in vices—does not know anything about the Source within. He constantly seeks from without, and he's unconscious, unaware that the source is within himself.

The entire Universe, or if I'm allowed to say, God, is in all things and all beings in each and every atom of matter. Knowing this sacred truth will remove and burn away ignorance, faults, sufferings, darkness and untruth—the miseries of all humanity.

Realizing this will illuminate, transfigure, and enliven us at the center of each thing and every being.

This marvelous unity of the universe will sweep us into the sublime currents of a true spiritual frontier, away from the limited narrow frames of conditioning.

The Source is within and without each and every one of us. In each being and in each world. In everything and every atom, the divine force is present.

It is every being's mission to manifest the divine presence. For that to happen, one must evolve and be conscious of the Divine Presence in themselves. Each one of us must come to the point where they perceive the divine dwelling within, a resplendent Being, pure, who is neither born nor dies, and is all-powerful.

The divinity never imposes himself nor makes any claim, menaces, blame, nor curses or condemns.

He offers himself in the heart of men and all beings and all things. He is at work incessantly in order to perfect without constraint, to repair with reproaches, to encourage without prejudice, with patience to enrich everyone with the treasures of love and wisdom and light. He works to nourish, to guard and protect, and counsel and console because he understands all and supports all, excuses and pardons all, hopes for and prepares all, carrying all in Himself as the Greatest Servant to all.

Until we can be like Him, a true humble servant to all, we must allow ourselves to be transformed by this Divine Love on every plane of our activities, thoughts and feelings without reservation in our marvelous organism.

To achieve this total consecration, perseverance is indispensable. To persevere in the right resolve to reach our goal. For every goal or endeavor, there will be sacrifices, challenges and obstacles. For those who run the rush of losing confidence and courage, take to heart the lessons that brings forth the message of hope. For there is no night without day-break. When darkness is at its thickest, dawn is ready. There is no fog that the sun does not dissipate, no tears that did not dry, no cloud that does not gild. There is no snow that does not melt, no winter that does not change into radiant spring, no storm that does not bow to the rays of light.

All things bring forth a counterpoise of glory. There is no distress that cannot be transformed into joy, no defeat that does not turn into victory, no downfall that does not change into an ascension to greater heights. There is no solitude that does not becomes a very home of life, no discord that is not resolved by harmony.

How close is he to the summit who awakes in the depths, for the deeper the abyss, the more the height reveals itself.

One who has sunk into the abysm of sufferings, the Divine affection, the Supreme benediction, will receive you for you have passed through the crucible of purifying sorrows for you are the glorious ascent.

During the wilderness and turbulences of your life, pause for a moment, and listen to the silent voices that will gladden your soul, awakening your spirit to the divine harmonies within you.

In the deep of the night, gather the priceless treasures of darkness, the creatures of light, for the night is filled with shining stars that have pure white luminosities, and they light up the hidden road of perfection to the secrets of Spiritual riches.

We are following the way of plentitude. When we have nothing left, all will be given. For those who are sincere and honest, out of the worst emerges the best. Any adversary that rages against man to annihilate him, serves only to make him greater. No state is ever so precarious as when man separates himself from his divine source. The universe, the source and cause of all causes, the most complete and perfect, watches over the horizon of things.

Since man could not climb or reach the source of life, the Universe's cosmic intelligence, sprung up within him. Since he could no longer receive the light from high, the Light shines forth from the very center of his being. Since man could not commune with transcendental love most high, the divine gave himself an offering dwelling within each human ego and his sanctuary.

The Will of our divine presence is deep within us, so that matter that may have been deemed despised and desolate, becomes fertile and blessed. Each atom contains a divine spark of thoughtforms, sensation, and gestures. Each being carries within himself a Divine Inhabitant within the entire Universe.

-Tian De

GLOSSARY

Yoga: The life pursuit of expanding one's experiential state of realization.

Chakra: Defined as wheel or lock, a junction point in the etheric body that when purified serves to amplify one's concentration.

Gomchen: Special individual in Tibet responsible for meditating day and night, with the purpose of capturing stray demons.

Dharma: Literally translated as teaching or work. However, the word refers to realization and is better understood as "learning through realization." The phrase, "the sage works for dharma," means the sage works for conscious realization/understanding.

Etheric Body: The Etheric body consists of the noetic, astral, and spiritual bodies of an individual.

Intelligence: The extent of the development of one's concentration, an aspect associated with experiential clarity and potential.

Dan Tien: Container of vitality water in the etheric body. Responsible for nourishing and empowering the physical body.

Self-Realization: An understanding of one's self that is gained through an expanded perception of reality.

BOOKS OF RELATED INTEREST

Enter Mo Pai: The Ancient Training of the Immortals – James Van Gelder

Magic and Mystery in Tibet - Alexandra David Neel

Changing Destiny: Liao Fan's Four Lessons

Initiation into Hermetics – Franz Bardon

Kundalini Yoga - Swami Saraswati Sivananda

Opening the Dragon Gate: The Making of a Modern Taoist Wizard – Chen Kaiguo

Ling Bao Tong Zhi Neng Nei Gong Shu – Wang Liping

The Magus of Strovolos – Kyriacos C. Markides

The Wandering Daoist - Deng Ming-Dao

The Magus of Java – Kosta Danaos

T'ai Chi Classics – Waysun Liao

BIBLIOGRAPHY

Bardon, F. (2013). *Initiation into Hermetics*. Holladay: Merkur Pub Company.

Belobragin, D. (2011). *Immortality in Taoist Alchemy, Levels of Achievements*. Retrieved from www.All-Dao.com: http://www.all-dao.com/immortality-achievements.html

Bilocation. (2016, April 3). Retrieved from Wikipedia: https://en.wikipedia.org/wiki/Bilocation

Brothers, T. W. (Director). (1999). *The Matrix* [Motion Picture].

C. G. Jung, R. W. (1962). *The Secret of the Golden Flower; A Chinese Book of Life*. NY: Mariner Books.

Carnagey, J. (n.d.). *The Pineal Gland in all Vertebrates*. Retrieved from Hermetic Source: http://www.hermeticsource.info/the-pineal-gland-in-all-vertebrates.html

Chadwick, D. (2016, April 8th). *Alan Watts*. Retrieved from http://alanwatts.com/

Chakras. (2006, 220).

Chakras. (2006, 2 20). Retrieved from Namaste: http://www.namaste.it/kundalini/kundalini_eng/chakras1.html

Chen Kaiguo, Z. S. (1998). *Opening the Dragon Gate: The Making of a Modern Taoist Wizard.* (T. Cleary, Trans.) North Clarendon: Tuttle Publishing.

Chenagtsang, D. N. (2014, September 24). The Rainbow Body, by Dr Nida Chenagtsang. *http://www.iattm.net.* Tibet. Retrieved from https://www.youtube.com/watch?v=QN9LR32-mWo

Chongyang, W. (1113 – 1170). *The Secret of the Golden Flower.* China: Wooden Tablet.

Coleman, G. (2007). *The Tibetan Book of the Dead.* London: Penguin Classics.

Danaos, K. (2000). *The Magus of Java: Teachings of an Authentic Taoist Immortal.* Rochester, Vermont , United States of America: Inner Traditions.

Dass, R. (2015). *Ram Dass Gives Maharaji the "Yogi Medicine".* Retrieved from Ram Dass: www.ramdass.org

David-Neel, M. A. (1971). *Magic and Mystery in Tibet.* Mineola, New York: Dover Publications.

Fan, L. (n.d.). *Liao Fan's Four Lessons.* Buddha Dharma Education Association Inc.

Flanagan, P. (1998, May 10). *SF Tesla Society Patrick Flanagan.* Retrieved from https://www.youtube.com/watch?v=gd-52ZeMq_4

Haiduk, S. (2015). Brains on Trial. *Imperial College of London.*

Harji, H. (2013, April 30). Siddhartha Gautam Becomes Lord Buddha. http://hariharji.blogspot.ca/.

Haughton, B. (2007, November). *Mind Power - Strange Cases of Suspended Animation* . Retrieved from Mysterious People: http://www.mysteriouspeople.com/suspended_animation.htm

Herbert, F. (n.d.). *Dune*. Penguin .

Hiinman, R. (2009, January 23). Shiva. *The destroyer and transformer.*

Horvatin, S. (n.d.). *Ophiuchus the Serpent Bearer*. Retrieved from pa.msu.edu: http://www.pa.msu.edu/people/horvatin/Astronomy_Facts/constellation_pages/ophiuchus.htm

Hua, H. (1974). *The Vajra Prajna Paramita Sutra*. Malaysia: Buddhist Text Translation Society.

Hua, M. H. (1974). *The Vajra Prajna Paramita Sutra*. Burlingame: Buddhist Text Translation Society.

Hudson, W. C. (2007). *Spreading the Dao, Managing Mastership, and Performing Salvation: The Life and Alchemical Teachings of Chen Zhixu*. Indiana.

Jnana. (2015, October 3). Retrieved from Wikipedia, the free encyclopedia: https://en.wikipedia.org/wiki/Jnana

Johnson, J. A. (2005). *Chinese Medical Qigong Therapy*. Retrieved from http://www.qigongmedicine.com/

Kohn, C. D. (2003). *Women in Daoism*. Three Pines Press.

Kohn, L. (1998). *Lao-Tzu and the Tao-Te-Ching*. New York: State University of New York Press.

Kung, V. M. (2005). *Changing Destiny: Liao-Fan's Four Lessons*. Taiwan: Corporate Body of Buddha Educational Foundation.

Leadbeater, C. W. (1927). *The Chakras*. London: The Theosophical Publishing House.

Luk, C. (1973). *Taoist Yoga*. England: Rider & Co.

Markides, K. C. (1989). *The Magus of Strovolos: The Extraordinary World of a Spiritual Healer*. London: Penguin Books.

Markides, K. C. (2001). *The Mountain of Silence: A Search for Orthodox Spirituality*. New York: Penguin Books.

Ming-Dao, D. (1986, October). *The Wandering Taoist*. Harper & Row.

Mouravieff, B. (1990). *Gnosis, Exoteric Cycle: Study and Commentaries on the Esoteric Tradition of Eastern Orthodoxy*. Praxis.

Mouravieff, B. (1990). *Gnosis, Exoteric Cycle: Study and Commentaries on the Esoteric Tradition of Eastern Orthodoxy*. Hermitage , TN: Praxis Inst Pr.

Osho. (2014). *The Secret of Secrets*. Watkins Publishing.

Ouwerkerk, E. C. (n.d.). *Rainbow body*. Retrieved from Satsang and Darshan website: https://soonyata.home.xs4all.nl/sorubasamadhi.htm

Paspardo, C. a. (2007, April 6). Astronauts. *Zurla Area R1*. Nadro, Public Domain: Rock Art Natural Reserve of Ceto.

Peppers, R. H. (Director). (2012). *Californication Era* [Motion Picture].

Persinger. (2010). The Electromagnetic Induction of Mystical and Altered States Within the Laboratory. *Journal of Consciousness Exploration & Research*, 808–830.

Ping, W. L. (29 March 2012). *Ling Bao Tong Zhi Neng Nei Gong Shu*. (R. Liao, Trans.) Printed by CreateSpace.

Potanin, N. (2013). Neijing Tu Stele. *Diagram of the Internal Texture of Man*. Beijing, China.

Rhodes, H. (1919). *Psychoma*. Kessinger Publishing.

Rinpoche, K. T. (n.d.). *The Six Paramitas - Phar-phyin-drug*. Retrieved from Rinpoche: http://www.rinpoche.com/teachings/paramitas.htm

Sadhguru. (2015, May 8th). Sadhguru - 7 Chakras Explained. India: Isha Foundation. Retrieved from https://www.youtube.com/watch?v=7IhcstEIvSs

Schipper, K. M. (1993). *The Taoist Body*. University of California Press.

Shang-yen, M. (1985, December 22). *The Five Eyes*. Retrieved from Chan Newsletter: http://chancenter.org/cmc/1987/10/08/the-five-eyes/

Shen, D. C. (1984). The Five Eyes. New York: Chinese American Forum.

Sheng-Yen, M. (1987, October 22). *The Five Eyes*. Retrieved from Ch'an Newsletter-No.62: http://chancenter.org/cmc/1987/10/08/the-five-eyes/

Shepard, J. (2004, May 6). Jesus Christ empowered by the Holy Spirit.

Sivananda, S. (n.d.). *Kundalini Yoga*. Rishikesh, India: The Divine Life Society.

Smoley, R. (2002). *Inner Christianity: A Guide to the Esoteric Tradition*. Boston: Shambhala Publications.

Stevens, S. (2009, September 17th). The Vantage Petroglyphs. *Petroglyph*. Washington State. Retrieved from https://www.flickr.com/photos/earball/4033402762/

The Litany of Bodhidharma Bodhisattva. (n.d.). *Shasta Abbey*. Mt. Shasta, California.

Thoreau, H. D. (1854). *Walden*. Boston: Ticknor and Fields.

Toda, J. (2015). *Five Types of Vision*. Retrieved from Soka Gakkai International: http://www.sgilibrary.org/search_dict.php?id=702

Vylenz, D. (Director). (2003). *The Mindscape of Alan Moore* [Motion Picture].

Walewski, C. S. (2006). *A System of Caucasian Yoga* . Whitefish: Kessinger Pub Co.

Wilcock, D. (2015, Febuary 8th). Tibetan Rainbow Body. *Contact In The Desert The Synchronicity Key The Hidden Intelligence Universe*. Video Presentation: Divine Cosmos. Retrieved from https://www.youtube.com/watch?v=0yjM04PH56g

Wood, R. C. (n.d.). *Movement of the Soul through the Body*. Retrieved from Nine Ways: https://ravencypresswood.com/2015/07/16/movement-of-the-soul-through-the-body/

Yogananda, P. (1955). *Autobiography of a Yogi*. Rider.

NOTES

PART 1

Awakening

[1] (Sheng-Yen, 1987)
[2] (Markides, The Magus of Strovolos: The Extraordinary World of a Spiritual Healer, 1989), Pg. 9

The Bhavacakra

[ii] Tibetan six realms painting from collection.
[1] Shakyamuni Buddha
[2] (Kung, 2005)
[3] (Rinpoche, n.d.)
[*] Philosophical question pondered among initiates in Tibet. Adapted from Alexandra David-Neel's book Magic and Mystery in Tibet.

Intelligence and Intellect

[1] (David-Neel, 1971), pg. 55
[2] (Jnana, 2015)
[3] (Chadwick, 2016)

Psychedelics

[4] A life pursuit focused towards developing the experiential quality.
[5] (Haiduk, 2015)
[6] (Dass, 2015)
[7] (Peppers, 2012)

PART 2
The Foundation

[1] (Rhodes, 1919), pg. 53
[2] (Markides, The Magus of Strovolos: The Extraordinary World of a Spiritual Healer, 1989), pg.64
[3] (Herbert)
[4] (Brothers, 1999)
[5] (Fan)
[6] (Markides, The Magus of Strovolos: The Extraordinary World of a Spiritual Healer, 1989), Page. 59
[1] (Danaos, 2000), pg. 123
[2] (Osho, 2014)
[3] (Fan)
[4] (Ming-Dao, 1986), pg.238
[5] (Kung, 2005)
[6] (Fan)
[1] TD is referring to becoming a Buddha.

Natural Progression

[1] (Markides, The Magus of Strovolos: The Extraordinary World of a Spiritual Healer, 1989), pg. 60
[2] (Markides, The Magus of Strovolos: The Extraordinary World of a Spiritual Healer, 1989), Page. 56
[3] (Ping, 29 March 2012)
[4] (Chen Kaiguo, 1998), Pg. 14
[5] Idea presented by fictional character Tyler Durden in Warner Brother's film Fight Club (1999).
[6] (Markides, The Magus of Strovolos: The Extraordinary World of a Spiritual Healer, 1989), pg. 49
[7] (Sivananda)
[8] (Vylenz, 2003)

The Etheric Body

[1] Sketch by Olivia Freemont
[2] The subtle dimension of one's self. The Etheric body consists of the noetic, astral, and spiritual bodies of an individual.

[3] (Flanagan, 1998), Time: 2:30:00

[4] (Chakras, 2006)

[5] (Horvatin, n.d.)

[6] (Carnagey, n.d.)

[7] Tibetan Chakra painting from private collection.

[8] Seven Seals image licensed under creative commons.

[9] (Bardon, 2013)

[10] (Shepard, 2004)

[11] (Harji, 2013)

[12] (Hiinman, 2009)

[13] (Paspardo, 2007)

[14] (Stevens, 2009)

[15] (Markides, The Mountain of Silence: A Search for Orthodox Spirituality, 2001)

[16] (Persinger, 2010)

[17] (Potanin, 2013)

Post Neijing Tu Diagram

[1] (Schipper, 1993):100-112

[2] (Kohn C. D., 2003):184

[3] (Ming-Dao, 1986), pg. 116

[4] (Sadhguru, 2015)

[5] (Sadhguru, 2015)

[6] (Sivananda)

[7] (Sadhguru, 2015)

Activating the Etheric Body

[1] (Sivananda)

[2] Images provided by Spiritual Reality - The Journey Within, a highly recommended film on spiritual development. Website: http://www.spiritual-reality.com/

[3] This is a yogic technique where one stares at a candle flame for a period of time and then closes their eyes and stares at the after-image of the flame.

[4] (Danaos, 2000), pg. 144

[5] The writings of Herodotus.

[6] (Danaos, 2000)

[7] (Yogananda, 1955)
[8] (Haughton, 2007)
[9] (Haughton, 2007)
[10] (David-Neel, 1971)
[11] (Bardon, 2013)
[12] (Danaos, 2000)

Lu Dogbin 100 Character Tablet

[1] (Kohn L. , 1998), pg. 96
[2] (Kohn L. , 1998)
[3] Also known as Khechari Mudra by the Indian sages.

Alchemical Evolution

[1] Duff, L. T. (2009, June 10th). Gampopa's Mahamudra The Five Part Mahamudra of the Kagyus. *Padma Karpo Translation Committee* . Kathmandu , Nepal., Page. 36
[2] Sell, W. (2015). *The Secret of the Golder Flower.* Retrieved with permission from *http://thesecretofthegoldenflower.com*

[3] (The Litany of Bodhidharma Bodhisattva), Page. 3
[4] (Osho, 2014)
[5] Musical composition on Bhodidharma's teachings by Dr. Croft.
[6] (Chen Kaiguo, 1998), Reprinted with permission of publisher. Page. 22

Alchemical Methods

[1] Geometric diagrams used to stare at in order to harmonize the mind and become balanced.
[2] (See: "Initiations and Initiates in Tibet, pg. 77." Each sound and its color association with the chakras.)
[3] (Walewski, 2006)
[4] (Walewski, 2006)
[5] (Walewski, 2006)
[6] (Walewski, 2006)
[7] (Mouravieff, Gnosis, Exoteric Cycle: Study and Commentaries on the Esoteric Tradition of Eastern Orthodoxy, 1990)
[8] (Thoreau, 1854)

[9] (Danaos, 2000)

PART 3
The Remnants of Alchemy

[1] (Coleman, 2007)
[2] (Coleman, 2007)
[3] (Coleman, 2007)
[4] (Danaos, 2000)
[5] (Coleman, 2007)
[6] (Chen Kaiguo, 1998)
[7] (David-Neel, 1971), pg. 28
[8] (Bilocation, 2016)
[9] (Chongyang, 1113 – 1170)
[10] (Chen Kaiguo, 1998), pg. 143
[11] (Markides, The Magus of Strovolos: The Extraordinary World of a Spiritual Healer, 1989)
[12] (Chen Kaiguo, 1998)
[13] (Markides, The Magus of Strovolos: The Extraordinary World of a Spiritual Healer, 1989)
[14] (C. G. Jung, 1962)
[15] (Danaos, 2000)

Rankings of Consciousness
Ascension in Daoist Alchemy

[1] (Ping, 29 March 2012)
[2] (Ping, 29 March 2012) pg. 218
[3] (Hudson, 2007)
[4] (Ping, 29 March 2012), pg. 221
[5] (Markides, The Magus of Strovolos: The Extraordinary World of a Spiritual Healer, 1989) pg. 121
[6] (Chen Kaiguo, 1998)
[7] (Belobragin, 2011)
[8] (Danaos, 2000)
[9] (Markides, The Magus of Strovolos: The Extraordinary World of a Spiritual Healer, 1989), pg. 116
[10] (Markides, The Magus of Strovolos: The Extraordinary World of a Spiritual Healer, 1989)

Eastern Christianity – The Royal Way

[1] (Mouravieff, Gnosis, Exoteric Cycle: Study and Commentaries on the Esoteric Tradition of Eastern Orthodoxy, 1990)

[2] (Mouravieff, Gnosis, Exoteric Cycle: Study and Commentaries on the Esoteric Tradition of Eastern Orthodoxy, 1990)

[3] As explained by Jared W.

[4] (Mouravieff, Gnosis, Exoteric Cycle: Study and Commentaries on the Esoteric Tradition of Eastern Orthodoxy, 1990)

[5] The "centers" are also often referred to as bodies.

[6] (Mouravieff, Gnosis, Exoteric Cycle: Study and Commentaries on the Esoteric Tradition of Eastern Orthodoxy, 1990)

[7] (Mouravieff, Gnosis, Exoteric Cycle: Study and Commentaries on the Esoteric Tradition of Eastern Orthodoxy, 1990)

[8] (Mouravieff, Gnosis, Exoteric Cycle: Study and Commentaries on the Esoteric Tradition of Eastern Orthodoxy, 1990), pg. 60

[9] (Smoley, 2002)

[10] *The Golden Book*, quoted in Gnosis by Boris Mouravieff, vol. 2, pg. 254.

[11] (Mouravieff, Gnosis, Exoteric Cycle: Study and Commentaries on the Esoteric Tradition of Eastern Orthodoxy, 1990)

The Five Eyes of Buddha

[1] (Sheng-Yen, 1987)

[2] Capitalization is for distinction.

[3] (Sheng-Yen, 1987)

[4] (Sheng-Yen, 1987)

[5] The Surangama Sutra

[6] (Hua H. , 1974)

[7] (Hua H. , 1974)

[8] (Luk, 1973), pg. 159

[9] (Hua H. , 1974)

[10] Buddhist term meaning countless universes.

[11] (Toda, 2015)

[12] Defined: Duty/Teachings

[13] (Shen, 1984)

[14] (Hua H. , 1974)

[15] (Toda, 2015)
[16] (Hua M. H., 1974)

Ascension in Tibetan Buddhism

[1] (David-Neel, 1971)
[2] (Ouwerkerk, n.d.)
[3] (Wilcock, 2015)
[4] (Wilcock, 2015)
[5] (Ouwerkerk, n.d.)
[6] (Chenagtsang, 2014)
[7] (Ouwerkerk, n.d.)

All quotes by Tian De are included in the book with direct permission.

www.JamesVanGelder.com

35130081R00112

Made in the USA
San Bernardino, CA
15 June 2016